# Walt Disney World
# Step-by-Step
## 2020

A Common-Sense Planning Guide

## Sarah Hina

D1113331

**Theme Park Press**
*The Happiest Books on Earth*
www.ThemeParkPress.com

Although every precaution has been taken to verify the accuracy of the information contained herein, no responsibility is assumed for any errors or omissions, and no liability is assumed for damages that may result from the use of this information.

Theme Park Press is not associated with the Walt Disney Company.

The views expressed in this book are those of the author and do not necessarily reflect the views of Theme Park Press.

Theme Park Press publishes its books in a variety of print and electronic formats. Some content that appears in one format may not appear in another.

Editor: Bob McLain
Layout: Artisanal Text

ISBN 978-1-68390-220-1
Printed in the United States of America

**Theme Park Press | www.ThemeParkPress.com**
Address queries to bob@themeparkpress.com

*For Paul, Caroline, and Alex*

# CONTENTS

# Introduction

I fell in love with Walt Disney World on our first family trip in 2008, when our children were tiny and their wonder felt larger than life.

Sometimes, as it turns out, the magic is real.

Many trips later, that love for the Mouse has blossomed into a full-time career as an author and Disney travel agent. And while our daughter and son are now teenagers, and more inclined to choose a ride on Space Mountain over Peter Pan's Flight, their enthusiasm for our vacations has never wavered in the years since they first hummed along to "It's a Small World." Walt Disney World has become our family's home away from home—familiar, yet still full of endless delights that surprise and astound us.

And like any home, our loyalty gets tested on occasion. For while I dearly love the drop on Splash Mountain, eating Dole Whips in Adventureland, meeting Goofy on Main Street U.S.A., and ending our night by watching fireworks explode over Cinderella Castle, I don't love long lines, crowds, paying too much for meals and feeling overwhelmed by the need to micromanage what's supposed to be a family vacation.

If you're here because you're stressed about any of those things: welcome. You've come to the right place. Planning a Walt Disney World vacation—particularly in the months following the opening of Star Wars: Galaxy's Edge—should be exciting, and not scary. The key is to take things step-by-step.

My aim for this planning guide is simple: by the end of your trip, I want you to love Walt Disney World as much as my family does, and the way to do that is to avoid the traps so many first-time and repeat visitors fall into—either by preparing too little, and getting blindsided upon your arrival in the parks, or by planning too much and forgetting to have fun in the process.

Over the years, I've researched and perfected proven methods for minimizing wait times while touring the four theme parks, discovered which resort accommodations offer the best perks and most desirable amenities, learned how to score the hardest-to-get Walt Disney World dining reservations, and arrived at some simple tricks for sticking to a budget when you're in a place that seems designed, at every turn, to take your money. And much, *much* more.

And now I'd love to share what I've learned with you.

## What This Book Isn't

While I'd love to give you a rundown of each ride, attraction, and show to be enjoyed at Walt Disney World, this book will avoid lengthy descriptions of most attractions out of a simple need to streamline the content. Instead, I'll encourage you to peruse the Disney website to explore the various attractions, or visit YouTube to capture an up-close look at other Walt Disney World experiences.

What I will do is tell you the most efficient way to tour the attractions in each park, and which experiences to prioritize, and when.

This book isn't going to reflexively parrot Disney's notion of what a successful Walt Disney World vacation looks like, either. While I am a Disney fan, and loyal to the parks, I also have my issues and critiques. So if I think there's something you can skip, and save some money in the process, I'll say so, without reservation.

## Ride vs Attraction

What's the difference between a Walt Disney World ride and attraction, anyway? While these terms are often used interchangeably, I use the word ride when I'm talking about an attraction guests board that moves in some way. While all Walt Disney World rides are Disney attractions, not all attractions are Disney rides.

For instance, the Enchanted Tiki Room at Magic Kingdom is an attraction, but not a ride, since guests sit in a room watching an animatronic performance. It's a small distinction, but one that provides some nuance.

Just don't ask me to categorize the classic Magic Kingdom stage show, Carousel of Progress. Guests sit in a theater, so it must be an attraction, right? But wait—the theater rotates throughout the show, meaning the guests are technically moving!

I suppose there's an exception to everything.

## The Four Theme Parks

Although there's a lot more to Walt Disney World than just the four theme parks, they remain most vacationers' touring priority when visiting Orlando. So let's get familiar with them.

**MAGIC KINGDOM** is what usually springs to mind when people think about Walt Disney World, with nostalgic Main Street backed by the soaring spires of Cinderella Castle. And for good reason! Magic Kingdom was the first park to open in 1971, and endures today as the most popular Disney theme park in the world, drawing 21 million annual visitors through its gates. There are far more attractions here than at any other Walt Disney World destination, distributed throughout six classic lands: Main Street, U.S.A., Tomorrowland, Fantasyland, Liberty Square, Frontierland, and Adventureland. For young children—and the young-at-heart—there is simply no place in all of Walt Disney World that exerts the same attraction or pull, and for parents of young kids, you may count on spending 40–50% of your time at this most magical destination, which boasts the ultimate in rides, Disney character meet-and-greets, parades, fireworks, shopping, and dining.

**EPCOT** (Experimental Prototype Community of Tomorrow) was the next park built on Walt Disney World property, in 1982, and remains a sentimental favorite with many guests. Why? Maybe it has something to do with the fact that Walt Disney intended for Epcot to be a functional city, drawing on American innovation and new technology to create a kind of modern utopia. Although he died before construction began, you can see Walt's original mission take shape in Future World, where design, human aspiration, and the living sciences come together to create dynamic worlds of imagi- nation and play. But Epcot has another half, situated across from the giant "golf ball" that's so iconic to the park: World Showcase. Here you can explore a kind of permanent World's Fair throughout unique pavilions paying tribute to eleven countries' cultures, all situated around a tranquil lagoon from which fireworks explode each night. World Showcase may be light on rides, but it's the best place in any theme park to just relax and enjoy a good meal, all while soaking up a rich, vibrant atmosphere.

**DISNEY'S HOLLYWOOD STUDIOS** is the destination that's seen the greatest evolution from its opening day in 1989, from being the theme park that boasted a functional production studio with a backlot guests could tour, to its present incarnation as a destination that celebrates artistic achievements in film, television, music, and theater. Coming on the heels of Toy Story Land's 2018 inauguration, 2019's opening of Star Wars: Galaxy's Edge exploded expectations for what a theme park experience could offer its guests. While I'm impressed by Hollywood Studios' recent growth and awed by its Imagineers' vision, I love it most for its beautiful evocation of 1930s–1950s Hollywood, with all the attendant glamour and spectacle that image conjures.

Walt Disney's sketches of Mickey Mouse, taken from
One Man's Dream in Disney's Hollywood Studios.

**DISNEY'S ANIMAL KINGDOM** was the last Walt Disney World park to open, in 1998. It's themed around the worlds of wildlife and habitat conservation, with a spectacular safari experience that's the next best thing to crossing the savannas of Africa yourself. Once dubbed a "half-day park" due to a relative paucity of rides, the unveiling of Pandora: The World of Avatar in 2017 has changed all that, opening the floodgates to new visitors keen to claim a role in this highly imaginative, uniquely Disney dreamscape. The park has always been a favor- ite of children who love the wildlife trails and the excellent, Broadway-style shows. To my mind, Animal Kingdom is the most magnificently themed of all Walt Disney parks and is certainly deserving of the new love and attention being lavished on it.

What about the other destinations found throughout the Walt Disney World resort? We'll get to those in due course.

## Getting Started

Enough introductions! After all, it was Walt Disney himself who once said: "The way to get started is to quit talking and begin doing."

Let's get doing.

Let's plan your Walt Disney World vacation.

# Choosing the Length and Dates of Your Trip

When should you visit Walt Disney World for the best possible vacation experience? And what's the ideal length of stay for most travelers?

First, a reality check: if you have kids who can't miss school for a trip to Walt Disney World, your choice of travel times will be limited. That's not to say you should take your kids out of school so that they can enjoy a less crowded vaca- tion experience. Missing school is a personal choice every family must make. But with a smart touring strategy (discussed in Step Ten), you can accomplish nearly everything you want to at all four theme parks—even during the busiest week of the year.

Now let's take a closer look at a subject of great concern to most Walt Disney World vacationers: park crowds.

## Crowds

Nobody wants to spend a costly vacation standing in line. (Even if Disney's queues are the best-themed, and well air-conditioned, in the world.) So when should you plan a trip that skirts the 90-minute wait for Space Mountain? The answer isn't as obvious as it used to be, as Disney has grown quite adept at spreading out its crowds through the touring seasons. That's ultimately a good thing, because it means that some of its busier times, like summer, have become a little less so of late.

Yet distinctions still exist between slow and busy weeks at Walt Disney World. First, let's discuss the absolute worst times to visit Walt Disney World, in terms of crowds:

**CHRISTMAS/NEW YEAR'S WEEK.** This is Walt Disney World's busiest week. To manage crowd flow, Magic Kingdom will occasionally close its gates. If you've always wanted to know what it would feel like to be trapped inside a champagne bottle—just squeeze yourself between twenty of your favorite strangers at Epcot on New Year's Eve, waiting for the fireworks to pop.

**SPRING BREAK.** Because of schools' differing spring break schedules, Disney World will see an influx of crowds starting the second week of March and peaking Easter week.

**JULY 4.** The busiest weekend of the summer season.

**EARLY NOVEMBER.** The overlap of the Wine & Dine Half Marathon, Jersey Week, and Epcot's Food & Wine Festival makes this a surprisingly busy time at Walt Disney World.

**THANKSGIVING.** Not as bad as Christmas week, but bad enough. Guests begin streaming into the parks on the Monday before Thanksgiving and often stay until the Sunday beyond.

**THREE-DAY WEEKENDS.** A lot of people think Martin Luther King Jr., Presidents' Day, and Columbus Day weekends are perfect opportunities to squeeze in a quick Disney vacation. Again—a lot of people think this.

So when are the best times to visit for lighter crowds? Historically, these weeks have seen lower attendance at Walt Disney World:

- Late January to early February
- Late February to early March
- Late April to mid-May
- Late August
- September
- Mid-November
- The first two weeks of December

If I had to pick a single best time to visit Walt Disney world for low crowds, I'd pick the month of September. Here's an important caveat, though: in the past two years, even the "low crowd" seasons have seen a surprising influx of guests, which makes future prognostications difficult. This is especially

Big Thunder Mountain Railroad will develop some of
Magic Kingdom's longest lines on busier days.

true with the opening of Star Wars: Galaxy's Edge in 2019. So
what does all this mean for you? Weigh other factors into your
decision-making process more than park attendance. Because
right now, people are going to Walt Disney World in record
numbers—at every time of the year.

## Weather

Maybe you've heard, but it gets hot in Orlando.

Starting in May, temperatures climb into the 90s and stay
there, with few reprieves, until the end of September brings
a modicum of relief. Florida's humidity adds another (oppres-
sive) layer to the story. In fact, word has gotten around that
summer touring at Walt Disney World's theme parks—where
you may walk 6–10 miles a day—presents some unique challenges, which may partially explain recent summers' lower
attendance numbers.

It does get hot in the parks. It will drain you. I've been to
Walt Disney World in August and I can attest that you do, in
fact, sweat through your clothes within the first half-hour of
park touring. Here's the silver lining, though: Disney World is
not Six Flags or Busch Gardens. You will spend a lot more time

in air-conditioned queues, stores, and restaurants than you do at other theme parks. This goes a long way toward making a summer trip bearable. It also helps to take a mid-afternoon break at your resort during the hottest time of the day, when—strangely enough—the parks' lines are also longest.

The upside to Orlando's tropical latitude is that you can swim at your resort year-round—though doing so demands a hardier constitution in December and January, when evening temperatures can drop into the forties. This is a big boon to spring breakers eager to soak up that beautiful Florida sunshine after enduring those dark, frigid winters up north. Granted, one of Walt Disney World's water parks will usually close for refurbishment during the winter season, but the other one will remain open for guests requiring their quota of lazy river time.

*Note*: The heart of Florida's hurricane season runs from late August to early November. While it is inherently riskier to book a vacation during this time, remember that Disney has only closed its theme parks about once per decade due to hurricane activity. You will see a high volume of thunderstorms during any summer visit, though. Be sure to purchase travel insurance for extra peace of mind.

## Park Hours

An often overlooked consideration when planning a Walt Disney World vacation is how long the parks remain open each night. Disney carefully calibrates park hours to match the expected number of visitors each day. It simply doesn't make financial sense for them to keep Magic Kingdom open until midnight at the beginning of February, when crowds are sparser. Yet for Christmas week, and during spring break, it's essential to keep the parks running from early in the morning until late at night to placate guests—from families with young kids who will do most of their park touring early in the day, to couples or families with teens who might be most eager for a nighttime park experience.

What this means for you depends a lot on your sleeping habits. But hypothetically, it's possible to get just as much done during a "high-volume" week such as spring break, or

Thanksgiving, as it is during a slower time of the year. You'll simply want to take advantage of the extended morning and nighttime park hours, while escaping the worst of the crowds in the heart of the day for some much needed pool or nap time. If you're a late riser, it's going to be challenging to do everything you want during low-volume times when the parks may close as early as 8:00 in the evening. Alternatively, if you're an early bird who conks out at 9:00 each night, bear in mind that you're not likely to find those 1:00am Magic Kingdom closing times very valuable.

It's also worth mentioning that Disney will typically feature more entertainment options during its busier times of the year: this means more parades, more firework shows, and more live entertainment for you to enjoy, in spite of the heavier crowds.

*Note*: Although Disney will release its park hours six months in advance of your stay, these are estimates only. Hours aren't solidified until a couple weeks before a visit, making long-range planning tricky. That being said, closing times change more frequently than openings, and are almost always pushed back, allowing visitors more time to enjoy that park's entertainment. Epcot's park hours are least prone to changes. Magic Kingdom's evening hours are the most frequently expanded.

## Ride Refurbishments

With four theme parks—and dozens of attractions to enjoy—it's not likely you'll plan a trip to Walt Disney World around the closure of a single ride. Yet it's worth looking up scheduled attraction refurbishments so you can adjust your—and your children's—expectations accordingly. If you've been looking at online ride videos with your kids to ramp up their excitement in advance of your trip, you don't want them feeling crestfallen when they finally arrive at Magic Kingdom, only to find that Splash Mountain is closed during the duration of your stay.

## Special Events

One of the reasons crowds are up during historically slower weeks is that Disney has grown innovative in creating novel, exciting reasons to explore the Walt Disney World resort during every month of the year. Whether it's a festival, a special night- time party, or a runDisney event, even park veterans are finding interesting ways to make Walt Disney World feel "new" again. And if this is your first trip to Walt Disney World, where everything is new, there could still be something listed below that catches your eye and makes the difficult choice of when to visit an easier one.

**JANUARY.** Falling shortly after New Year's, marathon weekend is the biggest runDisney event of the year, with races being run from Thursday through Sunday. Are you a runner? Need a reason to start? There's no motivation like running your first 5K, 10K, half marathon, or full marathon through a Disney theme park, with beloved Disney characters cheering you on. Not able to make it in January? Check the runDisney website (rundisney.com) for other races scheduled throughout the year.

**JANUARY/FEBRUARY.** The Epcot International Festival of the Arts is a rare opportunity to immerse yourself in Disney's storied past, with curated art exhibits featuring the work of real Disney Imagineers, workshops and seminars for guests to participate in, and a bevy of impressive musical performances featuring authentic Broadway talent. This is a newer event for Disney—and one that's already made a big splash.

**MARCH/MAY.** I make no bones about it: Epcot is my favorite park. And there is no better time to appreciate its special beauty than during the International Flower & Garden Festival. To mark the start of spring, thousands of flowers will bloom to life across Epcot's stunning gardens, fanciful topiaries, and special educational venues, with numerous opportunities to get your own hands dirty via seminars and demonstrations. Another perk of the Flower & Garden Festival is that over time, it's evolved into a smaller version of autumn's popular Food & Wine Festival, meaning springtime guests can also sample delicious food throughout World Showcase at the many outdoor kitchen booths. You might enjoy a favorite musical act during desig-nated nights, too, as part of the Garden Rocks concert series.

**LATE AUGUST/NOVEMBER 1.** Mickey's Not-So-Scary-Hal-loween Party (MNSSHP) is the rare opportunity to see Magic

Kingdom through new eyes, as kids (and adults) dress up to trick-or-treat, sample special snacks, ride favorite attractions, and meet some iconic—and more obscure—Disney characters. There's a spectacular parade and special fireworks show to enjoy as well. Unfortunately, not everyone can attend MNSSHP, as it's a special ticketed event starting at 7pm, after the park has been closed to regular visitors.

If you buy tickets for MNSSHP, and don't go to any other park that day, it will not count against your regular Walt Disney World ticket. In other words, if you were planning on purchasing a 5-day ticket, but want to attend the Halloween party—and are able to secure tickets for that event in advance—you might think about buying a 4-day ticket instead. Another big perk of buying into this event: you'll be allowed into Magic Kingdom at 4:00pm, despite the time stamp on your ticket. That's three more hours to enjoy Disney's most popular theme park! Knowing this, it might be the perfect day to visit a water park or explore Disney Springs, until you don your costume and become a participant in Disney's not-so-spooky story.

Topiaries greet Epcot's visitors during the International Flower & Garden Festival each spring.

*Note*: Even if you're not attending MNSSHP, it's wise to check the Disney website to find out which nights Magic Kingdom will be hosting the party. Here are two thoughts regarding Magic Kingdom visits on a party day:

- Visiting Magic Kingdom on MNSSHP days can be a good thing, especially if you have a Park Hopper ticket, since the park is typically less crowded due to its limited running hours. This means you may enjoy shorter lines in the park throughout the morning and afternoon, before being kicked out around dinnertime.

- If you have a Base ticket that restricts you to visiting one park per day, you will probably not want to use it at Magic Kingdom on a MNSSHP night, unless you'd be finished with the park by 6pm.

**SEPTEMBER/NOVEMBER.** Epcot's International Food & Wine Festival might be the most hotly anticipated event on Disney property, and is an excellent opportunity to savor delicious food and drinks from around the world in modest portions that beg for sampling and sharing with friends and family. The festival maintains an adult-friendly atmosphere and typically draws a lot of locals with its promise of new tastes, pleasant weather, and a more relaxed vibe. Celebrity cooking demonstrations, ticketed seminars and other exhibitions are also offered up for your enjoyment and learning, as is the popular Eat to the Beat concert series, featuring performers and bands both contem- porary and nostalgic. If you're on the Disney Dining Plan, think about using your snack credits at the kitchen booths, where costs mount quickly.

Try visiting the Food & Wine Festival on weekdays, as locals typically head there on Saturdays and Sundays. Fortunately, Future World is usually unaffected by Food & Wine's crowds. But by all means, avoid World Showcase during the first full weekend of November, when the Wine & Dine Half Marathon is being run. Outside of Christmastime, this is Epcot's busiest weekend.

**EARLY NOVEMBER/CHRISTMAS TIME.** Mickey's Very Merry Christmas Party is a ticketed, after-hours event held 2–3 times per week at Magic Kingdom, similar in format to

Mickey's Not-So-Scary Halloween Party. Besides special meet-and-greets with Disney characters, paying guests may enjoy hot cocoa and cookies, rides with shorter wait times, stage shows, a marvelous parade featuring the star of the season, Santa Claus, and a luminous holiday fireworks show that puts an exclamation point on the night's festivities.

These are pricey events to pay for (and get pricier the closer you are to Christmas) on top of Disney's regular admission, so again, consider paying for one less day on your Magic Your Way ticket to ease any strain on your budget, and be sure to show up at Magic Kingdom's entrance by 4pm to get the maximum value out of your ticket.

**LATE NOVEMBER/EARLY JANUARY.** There are many exceptional ways Disney celebrates Christmas and the holidays throughout its theme parks and resorts, and all make for a truly memorable stay. Although decorations in the parks and resorts start going up in early November, Thanksgiving marks the true kickoff to the holiday magic. If staying on Disney property, that's when you'll see the resorts pull out all the stops with their trees and decorations. Standout events at Epcot include the International Festival of the Holidays, which features World Showcase storytellers reflecting on their countries' cultural traditions, and the Candlelight Processional, a popular retelling of the Christmas story accompanied by music and celebrity narration. Don't miss the special holiday fireworks shows at this time of year, too. The highlight of it all? Magic Kingdom, featuring Cinderella Castle festooned in "dream lights," is the winter wonderland every kid (and kid-at-heart) dreams of.

## Cost

The least expensive time to visit Walt Disney World coincides with the least crowded weeks of the year, making a vacation at the end of January or the middle of September especially enticing when you begin crunching those vacation dollars in your head.

Airline rates spike around the holidays and other popular vacation times, though you can often nab a good fare during the summer months. Check historical prices for the flight route you use, and see how it varies month to month. Visit airfarewatchdog.com to be notified of the exact moment your flight's price takes a dive, so you can snatch up a cheap fare before it disappears.

The cost of a Walt Disney World resort room will be your biggest financial hurdle, if staying on Disney property. Disney offers larger room discounts—and more enticing "package deals"—as incentives to travel during off-peak times. Even if you're staying "offsite" from Disney property, you can expect to pay more for accommodations when the kids are out of school. To see this firsthand, let's take an example: a family of four staying at Disney's All-Star Movies Resort. This is what you can expect to pay on various nights of the year, in 2020 dollars

- End of January: $130
- Beginning of Spring Break: $192
- Easter Week: $227
- Peak Summer: $177
- Late August: $144
- Thanksgiving: $180
- Early December: $148
- Christmas Week: $240

It's easy to see you'll be spending nearly twice as much to stay at a Walt Disney World resort during Christmas week—and Easter—than you will during Disney's "Value" season. In fact, when you stack up the savings across a week-long vacation, it quickly becomes apparent that going to Walt Disney World around the holidays is a very costly present to gift oneself. That's not to say you shouldn't do it. It's just a reminder that while holiday vacations have the potential to be extraordinary, because of the extra magic Disney brings to bear, they are also more crowded and costly, as a rule.

*Note*: Disney may offer "free dining" to guests staying at a Walt Disney World resort during slower weeks of the year. What does this mean? In lieu of a room discount, guests will enjoy some version of Disney's Dining Plan for free. This is an extremely popular promotion, usually released in late spring for that year's summer and/or fall guests. Though not always the best value, many guests enjoy the idea of eating "for free" and not having to nickel-and-dime food costs while on vacation. We'll look more closely at "free dining" in Step Four.

## Length of Stay

When plotting the scope of a family vacation, we're often constrained by school and work schedules—not to mention our pocketbooks. That being said, there are a couple things to keep in mind when designing a Walt Disney World trip that are different from planning for other destinations. Namely: cost/day and the toll a Disney vacation can take on a person.

If staying offsite of Disney property, you may sometimes land a valuable "free night" offer when booking a certain number of nights at an Orlando hotel, helping to defray the cost of a longer trip. While this isn't the case with Disney resorts, there are still savings to be mined when breaking down the cost of a typical Magic Your Way ticket. Because Disney wants you to extend your vacation, they incentivize your stay by substantially dropping the cost of extra park days once you hit a 4-day threshold. So if you're wondering whether you can afford another day at Magic Kingdom, the answer is probably "yes," as long as you can handle the extra night's food and accommodations cost. The additional ticket day will only run you $10–$20/person.

The real risk you run in planning a short Walt Disney World vacation touches on my second point: a Disney vacation is simply more exhausting than other family vacations. Fun—yes. Otherwise, we Disney diehards wouldn't go back as often as we do. But it is surprisingly tiring, especially for little ones. When planning at home, it's easy to think you'll just "power through" and not schedule any downtime in an effort to do as much as possible and get your money's worth. Trust me: this is every first-timer's mistake. It sounds counterintuitive, but be sure to pencil in time to do nothing at all. This might mean sticking an entire day of relaxation into the middle of your vacation, when you'll most need a break. Your family may find the idea strange at first, but they will later thank you for your foresight.

So how long should a vacation last? My ideal Orlando vacation is 7–8 days, when just doing Disney, particularly for first-timers. That may seem like a long stay, but remember—two of those will be travel days, with limited park touring time. That leaves 5–6 full days to enjoy the theme parks and include some needed breaks in your itinerary. In this way, you can enjoy every park once, and repeat visits to your favorites, whether you have a base ticket or a Park Hopper. You may even enjoy the freedom to experience a water park, visit other Disney resorts, or shop and dine at Disney Springs.

If you don't have the luxury of a week-long vacation, a shorter stay is doable. It's just important to know, going in, that you won't get everything done you'd like to. (Having a Park Hopper ticket, discussed in Step Three, helps.) Don't make yourself feel badly about this! Have everyone in your travel party make up a list of "must-do" attractions and entertainment and dining activities for each park. Hit those first, make a note of what you couldn't get to, and relish the opportunity to be at the most magical place on earth with the people you love, for however much time you've carved out. And remember—one of the best things about Disney vacations is looking forward to the next one!

STEP TWO

# Booking Accommodations

There's no bigger decision to make when planning a Walt Disney World vacation than deciding where to stay. Because so much depends on guests' choice of accommodations, picking the right hotel can be a daunting choice for a first-time visitor. Just a quick check online will fill you with enough conflicting advice to make you wonder if this is really a vacation—or some kind of mental jujitsu you must master. It's hard to know where to start.

In truth, making an informed decision starts from a simple place: understanding the distinctions between staying "onsite"—at a Walt Disney-owned resort—as opposed to booking your lodging "offsite," at one of Orlando's other accommodations.

## Onsite vs Offsite

In this section, we'll focus on your unique circumstances, and whether the benefits of staying on property for your group outweigh the potential savings you'll mine in booking a room elsewhere. We'll also zero in on some smart ways to save you money, wherever your Disney dreams take you.

There are undoubtedly some major perks to booking a room with Walt Disney. Here are the most important:

- **FREE TRANSPORTATION.** If you're flying into Orlando's airport, there's no need to rent a car. Just hop aboard the Magical Express, Disney's complimentary bus service to all of its onsite resorts that includes luggage drop-off to your room. After checking into your resort, you'll be invited to use a combination of buses, boats, gondolas, and Disney's monorail service for your travel needs.

- **EXTRA MAGIC HOURS.** Being an onsite guest has its privileges, perhaps the most important of which is the ability to spend more time inside Disney's four theme parks. On different days throughout the week (check Disney's website for schedules), each park hosts Extra Magic Hours, during which time resort guests may either enter the park an hour earlier than offsite guests, or stay one or two hours longer before closing. This is a wonderful way to build in more park time with shorter lines, and it's all included in the room price. (For Fall 2019 guests who are visiting on the heels of Star Wars: Galaxy's Edge's opening, Disney has rolled out extended Extra Magic Hours in the mornings at Hollywood Studios, Animal Kingdom and Magic Kingdom.)

- **MAKE FASTPASS+ SELECTIONS EARLIER.** FastPass+ (FP+) is Disney's unique ride reservation system that allows you to skip the longest lines for Disney's most coveted attractions. Although every guest is limited to three FP+ selections, onsite resort guests may book their attraction reservations 60 days in advance, while offsite visitors must wait until 30 days prior to their arrival, giving onsite guests an advantage toward securing harder-to-get FP+ reservations.

- **THE "DISNEY BUBBLE."** There's no question about it: Disney is unmatched at telling a story. This philosophy is reflected in everything Disney touches, including its resorts. Though your personal experience will vary based on which "level" of Disney resort (Value, Moderate, or Deluxe) you book, each property comes with a big splash of Disney charm in their impressive visuals and fun furnishings—and never more so than during the holidays.

- **CHARGING PRIVILEGES.** Being an onsite guest lets you conveniently charge in-park purchases, such as food or souvenirs, directly to your room by using your free MagicBand, Disney's high-tech wristband that doubles as a guest ticket and online information portal.

- **DINING PLAN.** Walt Disney World offers visitors the option of purchasing one of three Disney Dining Plans when booking a vacation package—but only for its onsite guests. Although the cost-saving benefits of using a Dining Plan are debatable, many guests appreciate the idea of having their dining expenses taken care of ahead of their trip.

- **ADVANCE DINING RESERVATIONS (ADRS).** Every guest—onsite and offsite—is eligible to make restaurant dining reservations up to 180 days in advance of their trip. Yet onsite guests enjoy the extra incentive of being able to book all of their ADRs on the first day their booking window opens, instead of making selections a single day at a time, for the duration of their trip, like offsite guests do. When it comes to enjoying the most unique dining experiences Disney has to offer, this seemingly trivial advantage assumes a greater import.

- **PACKAGE DELIVERY.** Don't feel like lugging a bag full of souvenirs around the parks all day? Tell the cast member (all Disney employees are called "cast members") ringing up your purchase which resort you're staying at, and your package will find its way there by the end of the day.

- **FREE PARKING AT THE THEME PARKS.** If you're driving to Walt Disney World, or simply like the freedom of using a rental car to get around Orlando, you won't be charged $25/day to park at the Disney theme parks when staying on property. Unfortunately, Disney has started charging drivers for the privilege of parking at their resorts.

- **ALL-IN-ONE CONVENIENCE.** This is the guiding principle underlying Disney's unspoken promise to its resort guests: "We may charge more, but we'll make everything as easy as possible for you." And you know what? They usually do.

Now that we've talked about all the ways a Disney resort may outshine its offsite competitors, I'm afraid I have some bad news: booking a Walt Disney World resort room for your vacation will usually cost more money than booking a larger room at an offsite hotel, and could even cost more than renting a vacation home.

This might not come as a shock. After all, you want to vacation at Walt Disney World partly because of their sterling reputation for customer service. And that attention to detail comes with a price. The question is, are the perks worth the added expense? Possibly not, as we'll see below.

Staying offsite requires a little more planning, and may involve less magic, but there are advantages to booking accommodations outside the Disney bubble

- **MORE BANG FOR YOUR BUCK.** Because Orlando is a popular vacation destination, offsite hotels offer extremely competitive pricing. Often, you can book a two-room suite at a high-end hotel for the same price you'd pay for a Value or Moderate resort room on Disney property. This means your family can spread out, allowing for a better night's rest. Plus, there are many luxury four and five-star Orlando resorts which are just as lovely as any Disney hotel, offering a host of attractive amenities to their guests. Should you choose to stay at one, you're likely to spend less than you would for a standard room at a Disney Deluxe resort. Ultimately, booking offsite means you'll have more money in your pocket to spend elsewhere, or save.

- **FREEDOM.** Using Walt Disney World transportation exclusively has its drawbacks. The most common complaint among Disney's onsite guests is the time it takes to get from Point A to Point B, especially when it comes to sharing bus routes and "resort hopping." When you stay offsite, you're reliant only on yourself and your rental car (there are shuttle services at many offsite hotels to Walt Disney World, but these are less reliable).

- **LOYALTY PROGRAMS.** Most modern hotels have their own loyalty programs, designed to turn you into a faithful customer. AAA and military discounts might be offered, too. Accrued credit card points can also be a driving force in bringing down the cost of a room. When you choose to book with Disney, you're forgoing benefits accumulated throughout your purchasing year.

- **FREE BREAKFAST.** Food is a big expense at Walt Disney World. Even at a Value resort food court, you'll spend $5 for a kid's bowl of cereal with a cup of orange juice. Sure, you can bring food from home—or have groceries delivered to your resort for a charge—but at offsite hotels, you'll often find a hot, filling breakfast included in the room price. As a rule, you'll discover cheaper dining alternatives the more time you spend outside of Disney's reach.

- **CONVENIENT LOCATIONS.** Because the Walt Disney World resort is so massive, it's possible to find offsite hotels that are actually closer to your favorite Disney theme park than some onsite resorts. Even accommodations a little farther afield will likely cost you only a few minutes by car, especially when you factor in the slowness of some Disney transportation. Additionally, if you're planning on visiting other Orlando attractions, it might make more sense to book a room at a locale central to all of your touring plans, and not pay Disney rates for those nights when you can't benefit from many of the onsite perks.

- **CONDOS, HOMES, AND TOWNHOUSES.** It used to be that hotels were a family's only option when vacationing, unless they had a favorite aunt in town. Not anymore. With the proliferation of home-sharing sites like Airbnb, you can now book an apartment or home for the same price as a standard hotel room. Often, when renting a condo or townhouse from a site like VRBO or HomeAway, you'll even get your own pool thrown into the bargain. Plus, having access to a kitchen means you'll be able to buy groceries and prepare some homemade meals.

- **PETS.** Walt Disney World has started allowing dogs at select resorts—for a $50–$75/night fee. If you're traveling with Fido or Fluffy, you'll still find a greater selection of pet-friendly accommodations offsite.

- **PACKAGE PICK-UP.** Remember when I mentioned how great it was to have park souvenirs sent back to your Disney resort room? You can do nearly as well as an offsite guest. Just tell the Disney cast member checking you out that you want your item sent to Package Pickup, at a location convenient to each theme park exit.

- **DISNEY OVERLOAD.** I might not be the best person to make this argument, but I suppose it's possible to have too much of a great thing when it comes to experiencing Walt Disney World. Some guests find that at the end of the day, they just want to shake the pixie dust off their clothes and relax in a not-quite-so-magical space for a while.

Here are some additional considerations to help you decide whether to stay onsite or offsite:

- First-time visitors should stay onsite, unless your budget precludes it. I think it's worthwhile to get the full Disney experience the first time you visit Orlando, and you can find a reasonable rate by booking a Disney Value resort room. The first time our family visited Walt Disney World, we stayed at All-Star Movies, with four of us in a 260-square-foot room. The last time we went, we stayed at a two-bedroom offsite hotel suite, where the kids had their own beds, my husband and I enjoyed a king-sized mattress, and we made breakfast every morning in our kitchen before eating it on our outdoor balcony. We paid a similar rate for both accommodations. So do I regret that first stay? Not a bit. We had an absolute blast. Staying onsite was our best introduction to the immersive experience Walt Disney World provides. Even the parts that frustrated me—like being the last drop-off on our bus loop—were educational toward planning trips in the future. And our resort's theming made us that much more excited to get into the parks each day.

- Families with young children should also stay onsite. The first reason touches on my last point: Disney theming is so much fun for little ones to explore. I still remember the looks on our kids' faces when they saw the giant-sized Woody and Buzz Lightyear in our courtyard. Those moments don't come with price tags. All of Disney's Value resorts are designed with children in mind, boasting enormous Disney icons and fanciful room flourishes. Plus, the convenience of Disney transportation means you don't have to struggle with strollers or car seats when your kids conk out and you need to take them back to the resort for a midday nap. You'd be surprised at how easily kids can sleep in a stroller, even on a monorail.

- Travelers with different itineraries should stay onsite to make use of Disney transportation and not be tied to one rental car when compelled to split up. (Alternatively: you could use a taxi or rideshare to get you back to your offsite hotel if needed. Just be aware that most rideshare services charge quite a bit more for car-seat capability.)

- Large groups or families, by which I mean parties of six or more, should strongly consider staying offsite, because of the cost of booking two Disney resort rooms. There are larger suites and villas available at some Disney resorts, but they can get pricey. (Art of Animation and All-Star Music offer more reasonably priced suites. Some standard rooms accommodate five.)

- Members of the military would do well to consider a stay at Shades of Green, Disney's armed-forces recreation center that invites active service members and their families, in addition to Department of Defense employees and veterans, to enjoy Deluxe-style accommodations near Magic Kingdom for Value-sized prices. Keep in mind, however, you don't have access to the Disney Dining Plan or the Magical Express when lodging at Shades of Green, but you may enjoy Extra Magic Hours and other Disney transportation.

- Theme park commandos are people who spend nearly all their time at the theme parks, and only require a shower and bed upon stumbling into their rooms late at night. If you're someone who's not planning on being at the resort long enough to appreciate the theming or amenities, it's probably best that you stick with cheaper offsite lodging, instead of paying a premium for Disney-level ambiance and the more adventurous dining options offered at Moderate and Deluxe resorts. Although the Extra Magic Hours and FP+ booking advantage might appeal to a theme park commando, you'll likely have enough time at the parks to hit all the attractions, unless you've booked a shorter stay.

- Independent types should strongly consider staying offsite, or at least renting a car if rooming with Disney. If you're the kind of person who can't stand being inefficient with your time, and tire of being around people constantly, then don't make yourself wholly reliant on Disney transportation to shuttle you around.

- Guests with a lot of advance dining reservations will also find travel delays problematic if relying solely on Disney transportation, especially when dining at other resorts requiring convoluted bus routes. Resorts permit you to park in their lots when booking an ADR at one of their restaurants. And while there's no reason you can't rent a car while staying onsite (outside of Disney's resort parking fees), you will be forgoing one of the cost-saving benefits of rooming with Disney by doing so.

- Universal Orlando visitors should seriously consider staying at one of their onsite resorts, at least for that leg of the trip, to take advantage of their Express Pass offer.

- Camping enthusiasts will want to check out Fort Wilderness, Walt Disney World's beautiful, backcountry retreat, offering campsites and cabins in a wooded, wildlife-rich setting away from the hubbub of the parks—while still offering Disney amenities. Pets are permitted.

- For those wanting it both ways, why not do a split stay at a Disney resort and an offsite property? This creative solution requires a little more shuffling about, thus making the most sense for lengthier vacations, but doing so will cut the costs of staying entirely onsite while still letting you slip inside the Disney bubble for a while. This option is entirely possible within the Disney resort system, too! Desperately want to enjoy a night at Animal Kingdom Lodge, but can't swallow the cost of a weeklong stay there? Book a less expensive Value or Moderate resort room for six nights and save the last night for your "dream" resort. Cast members will ensure your luggage is delivered to your new resort room while you're out touring the parks for the day. Easy!

By now, I hope you have a pretty good notion of which accommodations will work best for your party.

# Choosing Your Disney Resort

Have you made the decision to stay with Disney? Let's break down their resort classes into a list of what you can expect to encounter as a guest there, in addition to highlighting the pros and cons of going Value, Moderate, or Deluxe. Later, we'll touch on the idea of renting DVC points from Disney's timeshare members (a clever workaround to enjoy Deluxe amenities at Moderate prices), talk about whether it's best to book a vacation package through Disney or shoot for a "room-only" discount, and briefly shine a light on the important topic of room requests. Finally, we'll look at a few of my personal resort recommendations for your Walt Disney World stay.

## Value Resorts

Because they're the most economical choice, and therefore most likely to interest young families new to Walt Disney World, we'll consider the Value resorts first: All-Star Music, All-Star Movies, All-Star Sports, Pop Century, and Art of Animation.

Value resorts are a great option for families who want to stay onsite cheaply, have young children who will love the fun theming and super-sized Disney figures, or for those guests who don't plan on spending a lot of time at the resort but desire Disney's onsite perks.

They are not a good choice for light sleepers, guests easily worn out by walking long distances, fine dining aficionados, large families (unless booking a more expensive suite), or adults longing for a semblance of luxury. These are motel rooms, for all intents and purposes. You can sleep in them, take a shower, and wind down at the end of a long day, but for all the lively theming, they are rather spartan in their space, furnishings, and amenities, especially when compared to standard American hotel chains like Holiday Inn or Hampton.

Every resort offers you the option of booking a "preferred room" for about $20 more a night, which gets you closer access to the main building, food court, and bus stop.

Which of the Disney Value resorts should you book? That's a highly subjective choice, but here are my top two picks based on theming, value, dining, and convenience.

**POP CENTURY.** Pop Century and Art of Animation have their own bus lines (during the off-season, the All-Star resorts must share), which cuts down considerably on transportation time, while also hosting a shared stop for Disney's new Skyliner system (discussed in Step Five). Pop narrowly wins my recommendation in this category based on its more compact layout, less crowded food court, and superior price point. Plus, Pop Century has completed room refurbishments that include the addition of queen beds, vinyl flooring and a coffee maker. Pop is a little more expensive than the All-Stars, with more understated room features—which could please or disappoint, depending on your enthusiasm for Disney flourishes. The overall theming of the resort takes its cues from 20th century pop culture. There are three colorful pools (all heated) in addition to splash pads for kids to play in, and a scenic running path lacing Hourglass Lake, which separates Pop Century from Art of Animation. Note: Pop too pricey for your trip dates? Check out All-Star Movies Resort, which is undergoing an impressive renovation that should be completed by the end of 2019.

**ART OF ANIMATION.** It's painful to rank Art of Animation second to anything—the resort's theming is just that good. Even after choosing Pop Century, you should take advantage of the resorts' close proximity to stroll the grounds of AoA, which features icons and murals from four popular Disney and Pixar films: Little Mermaid, The Lion King, Cars, and Finding Nemo. (Only the Little Mermaid building houses standard rooms; the other three buildings offer 6-person suites, situated closer to the main building and bus stop but costing considerably more.) Be sure to check out the Disney art in the resort's Animation Hall, and if you're hungry for something different, Landscape of Flavors is a notch above other food courts, featuring exotic flavors in addition to standard American fare. The main drawback to Art of Animation, though, is its huge, sprawling layout, which means that if you choose to book a standard room (the only true "Value" option), you'll be walking ten minutes or

Children staying at Disney's Pop Century Resort will
love seeing larger-than-life friends like Lady.

more to its one bus stop and food court. That said, its rooms are
slightly more spacious than other Value resorts. This, and the
fact that the resort boasts the best pools of all the Values, con-
tributes to its higher price point, but makes it worth a second
look when choosing an onsite stay, especially for large families
requiring suite-level accommodations.

## Moderate Resorts

The next step up from staying Value is booking a room at one
of Disney's five Moderate resorts, which run about $70 more
per night, while offering up more space, amenities, dining
options, and adult-friendly theming.

The five Moderate resorts are Caribbean Beach, Coronado
Springs, Port Orleans French Quarter, Port Orleans Riverside
and Fort Wilderness Resort & Campground. Let's break down
the benefits and drawbacks of choosing a Moderate as your
home base while vacationing at Walt Disney World, and dig
down into my top two picks in this category.

Disney's Moderate resorts are a "happy medium" choice
for people not wanting to spend an exorbitant amount of
money, but who still desire the more upscale, attractive room

features that can hold their own against most American hotel chains, and who will appreciate the lovely, transportive touches Disney brings to bear—whether that's through the more sophisticated dining options, a waterslide down a Mayan Temple, or an evening carriage ride.

Moderate resorts are not a great option for people who will spend little time at their resorts—Values remain the best option for these "theme park commandos." They're also not ideal for guests who believe the extra expense of a Moderate room will save them precious transportation time. I hate to tell you, but it probably won't. They are not likely to save you on steps, either, with the exception of Port Orleans French Quarter.

That being said, these are gorgeous properties, having some of the most passionate devotees in Disney guest surveys. Since I'm a moderate kind of person when it comes to most things, I'm also a fan, especially of these two properties, which take the prize as my top picks for Walt Disney World's Moderate resorts:

**PORT ORLEANS FRENCH QUARTER.** It's not any one thing that nudges Port Orleans French Quarter to the top of the Moderate heap; rather, it's a mix of attributes I find especially appealing for guests to Walt Disney World. First off, Port Orleans French Quarter requires the least amount of walking within the resort because it boasts the smallest layout and fewest buildings. This gives the resort a uniquely quaint and charming feel for a Moderate, making for a quieter stay. French Quarter bus service pulls it further ahead of the competition. There are times when the Port Orleans sister resorts must share a bus loop, in which case French Quarter guests will board first from one common stop, before proceeding to the four separate Riverside stops. But frequently French Quarter guests will enjoy their own separate line, making transportation more efficient than it is at other Moderates, especially Coronado Springs and Caribbean Beach. Want to visit Disney Springs, but feeling some serious bus fatigue? Enjoy a refreshing cruise down the Sassagoula River in your Port Orleans water taxi. Although I love the romantic ambiance Port Orleans Riverside conjures up, French Quarter's Mardi Gras palette is fun and cheerful and the landscaping as uniformly lovely as at all Disney moderates. The main drawback to Port Orleans French Quarter is its lack of a table-service restaurant, but with a recently renovated food court that benefits from a wide selection of tasty items, including its delectable New Orleans beignets, I don't think most families will pine for the lack of a finer dining option. If they do, they can walk the fifteen minutes to the excellent Boatwright's at Port Orleans Riverside.

**CORONADO SPRINGS.** Let me list the best (and possibly worst) thing about my second choice pick: it's the primary convention hotel at Walt Disney World. At first blush, then, it might not seem like the best choice for families, since many of its amenities are targeted at business-minded adults. But there are advantages to staying at a convention hotel from which everyone benefits, including beautifully updated rooms, an upscale food court, an onsite health club, a salon, room service, and several outstanding table-service restaurants. Situated around a 22-acre lake that stunningly reflects Florida's sunsets, Coronado's Spanish theming is lush and tranquil. The main pool is a standout for its size and Mayan waterslide and the playgrounds are more imaginative than

Swimmers can enjoy a slide down Scales, the Sea Serpent at the Port Orleans French Quarter feature pool.

most, making Coronado Springs a fine choice for children. Although the resort's layout is sprawling, its footprint is more negotiable than that of Caribbean Beach, especially with the new footbridges added in 2019, pursuant with the opening of Coronado's Gran Destino Tower, which now serves as the resort's welcome lobby. The only real downside to Coronado Springs is its numerous internal bus stops, and lack of secondary transportation options.

## Deluxe Resorts

If you're free from the pressures of sticking to a budget, have a special incentive to splurge on your vacation, or are planning on spending a lot of time relaxing and enjoying everything a Disney resort can offer their guests, then going Deluxe is the right choice for your Walt Disney World stay.

These are stunning properties, each themed to perfection, drawing inspiration from uniquely different sources. So make sure you explore the various styles of Deluxe resorts to see which speaks to you—personal tastes are most important when booking Deluxe accommodations because while one person might find the Grand Floridian's Victorian-era stateliness to be the last word in elegance, another might find it overly stuffy for her tastes. People's preferences vary wildly. When you're looking to spend this much money—Deluxe rooms start at $370/night and can quickly rise into the thousands of dollars for concierge-level indulgence—you should savor every moment of your stay.

What is universal throughout Disney's Deluxe properties is their undeniable "wow factor," outstanding dining establishments, luxury amenities, convenient kids' clubs, and elaborately designed pools and water features. Just be warned: when you go Deluxe, you're spoiling yourself for any other kind of future Disney vacation! If you're okay with that, I am, too.

While some Deluxe resorts are quite close to Magic Kingdom and Epcot, transportation will not always be quicker than it is from Disney's Values and Moderates. Some Deluxe resorts do share buses. Most offer a mix of transportation options, with only Animal Kingdom Lodge being wholly reliant on bus service. A lot of people think that paying more should mean less time spent sitting on a bus. While that's sometimes the case, Walt Disney World is just too big for any one resort to offer efficient transportation everywhere.

The best choice for families making frequent visits to Magic Kingdom is Disney's Contemporary Resort. While its theming is more understated than some Disney Deluxes, it has the enormous appeal of being a 10-minute walk to the most magical destination on all of Disney property. Plus, it's not every day you can see a monorail glide through your lobby!

The Deluxe resorts at Walt Disney World are the Contemporary Resort, Polynesian Village, the Grand Floridian Resort & Spa (these three are the so-called "monorail resorts"), Wilderness Lodge, Animal Kingdom Lodge, Beach Club, Yacht Club, and BoardWalk Inn. All of Disney's Deluxe resorts are individually compelling; there is no "average" experience to be found. So, rather than list a pair of "favorites," I will instead give you my choices for Best Value and Best All-Around Deluxe resort:

**BEST VALUE: WILDERNESS LODGE.** If you love the idea of returning to a serene National Park-inspired oasis after touring the theme parks, then the pristine beauty of the Wilderness Lodge was designed for your peace of mind. This resort's Pacific Northwest theming is my favorite among the Deluxe resorts, and the fact that you can enjoy its top-notch dining, outstanding pool and water features, and quiet, idyllic sanctuaries for the lowest price of all the Disney Deluxe accommodations should definitely turn your head. If you're visiting Walt Disney World during Christmas time, the Wilderness Lodge decorations are among the best on Disney property. A real touring advantage is found in the lodge's easy boat ride to Magic Kingdom. The resort is also boat buddies with the Contemporary and Polynesian resorts, convenient when booking popular dining reservations at both locations. Enjoying a longer stay? You can walk to Fort Wilderness for that property's numerous recreational programs. Buses will transport you to all other theme parks. The main downside of Wilderness Lodge is the smallness of its rooms, and their rather dark furnishings, compared to other Deluxe resorts.

Guests staying at Disney's Wilderness Lodge
will appreciate the resort's close proximity to
Magic Kingdom, and its secluded setting.

While Animal Kingdom Lodge is also spectacularly themed, and worth serious consideration if you're looking to spend less for a Deluxe stay at Walt Disney World, the necessity of paying more for a savannah-view room makes it a less attractive option, with the resort also being more isolated from the theme parks and its dining options less kid-friendly, overall.

**BEST ALL-AROUND: POLYNESIAN VILLAGE RESORT.** There's one Walt Disney World Deluxe resort that pops up more frequently on Disney diehards' "dream resort" lists than any other: the Polynesian (or "Poly," for short). That's for good reason: it has the most vacation-friendly theming of Disney's Deluxe resorts, rooted in the lushness of the South Pacific and Polynesian "Tiki" culture, is convenient for its monorail-stop location, has a wide variety of family-style dining options, boasts spectacular pools and white sand beaches ideal for nighttime fireworks viewing, and has a wide selection of spacious rooms (all of which include a sofa, reading chair, well-configured bathroom, and impeccable lighting). Last, but not least, the Poly is the only place outside of Magic Kingdom where you can get one of the most iconic snacks at Walt Disney

World: the Dole Whip! More seriously, if you want to immerse yourself in everything Disney has to offer, it would be hard to improve upon the Poly. In fact, with so much to do on property, you might find it hard to leave, though doing so is easy—for Magic Kingdom, just hop on a monorail or boat. And with a short walk to the Transportation & Ticket Center, you can ride to Epcot via monorail. (The Poly has its own bus system to Hollywood Studios and Animal Kingdom.) Want some private couple time while the kids have fun? The Poly has the most comprehensive childcare services on Disney property. Grab a drink with your partner at the fun, interactive Trader Sam's Grog Grotto before meeting up with the kids later to enjoy the Spirit of Aloha dinner show. Wake up early the next morning to meet Mickey, Pluto, Lilo, and Stitch at 'Ohana's family-style breakfast before setting out for the parks. The only downside to staying at the Poly? Sticker shock. It's one of the most expensive resorts on Walt Disney World property. It also books up fast, which says something for its appeal, so be sure to reserve a room months in advance when staying there.

Before moving on, I should mention two popular lodging options that blur the distinction between "onsite" and "offsite" hotels: the Swan and the Dolphin. These are architecturally eye-popping, high-end properties within walking range (or a quick boat launch) to both Epcot and Hollywood Studios, booked by guests wanting a less expensive room rate for a stellar location, luxury amenities, top-rate pools and dining, and other onsite Disney perks. So what are those benefits? Extra Magic Hours, free parking at the theme parks, package delivery to your room, and 60-day FP+ booking capabilities. What they won't offer you is access to Disney's Magical Express, free MagicBands, Disney Dining Plan add-ons and charging capabilities back to your room. Hotel shuttles will transport you to Magic Kingdom, Animal Kingdom, Disney Springs, and the water parks. While families may find the lack of Disney theming at the Swan and Dolphin hotels disappointing, their rooms are pleasantly spacious, their bedding downright sumptuous, and their prices competitive—just be prepared for those annoying resort fees to be tacked onto your bill at the end of the day.

For 2020, Walt Disney World has also extended its 60-day FP+ booking window and Extra Magic Hours to guests staying at select Disney Springs resorts: B Resort & Spa, Best Western Lake Buena Vista, DoubleTree Suites, Buena Vista Palace, Hilton Orlando Lake Buena Vista, Holiday Inn Orlando, and Wyndham Garden Lake Buena Vista. Because these properties are often well priced, and situated close to Disney Springs, they're worth a second look. Be aware that transportation is shared among these hotels, however, which can make for crowded shuttles and less consistent travel times.

*Note*: If you have your heart set on a certain view when booking your Disney resort room, or have requests concerning cribs, high chairs, bed rails, handicap accessibility, adjoining room connections, microwaves, balconies or room location, go to the "My Reservations and Tickets" section of your My Disney Experience account in the 60-day period leading up to your trip to make two room requests. For more specific inquiries, call 407-939-7630 ahead of your check-in date, or 407-9397807 for disability-related requests.

## Renting DVC Points

If you're like me, you'll have checked out some reviews and pictures of Disney's Deluxe resorts and started doing "Disney math" in your head, to make your budget stretch a little more in the mouse's favor. The truth is, not all of us can afford Disney's finest accommodations for this trip, and that's okay. Every onsite property has its charms, and you're going to have a fantastic vacation no matter where you stay on Disney property.

But if you keep feeling that pang of desire to go Deluxe, and think you can nearly swing the numbers, I'll give you one more option to consider: renting points from Disney Vacation Club (DVC) members.

Disney Vacation Club is a timeshare program in which members own "points" they use toward stays at Disney's Deluxe Villas. On occasions when they have points that are set to expire, members may rent points to outside buyers at comparatively low prices. It's not uncommon to see savings of 30-50% when renting points through accredited vendors like

David's Vacation Club Rentals and DVC Rental Store, both of which are backed by the Better Business Bureau, and possibly even more when you take the riskier route of renting points from individual sellers on online boards and forums.

Disney's DVC properties are the new Riviera Resort (opens December, 2019), Animal Kingdom Villas, Bay Lake Tower at the Contemporary, Beach Club Villas, BoardWalk Villas, Boulder Ridge Villas, Copper Creek Villas, Villas at Grand Floridian, Disney's Old Key West, Saratoga Springs Resort, Villas at Wilderness Lodge, and Polynesian Villas & Bungalows.

The advantages of booking DVC accommodations are the savings to the renter (that's you!); the fact that DVC Deluxe Villas are a great fit for large groups, since they come in studio, 1-, 2-, or 3-bedroom units; and the convenience you'll enjoy in being able to add on a Disney Dining Plan (and Magical Express transportation) without having to purchase theme park tickets through Disney. You might even do some cooking and laundry onsite—villas come with kitchens or kitchenettes in addition to a washer and dryer.

The main disadvantage is that your reservation won't be entirely within your control—you will have to rely on the DVC member to make your changes for you. Fortunately, by using an accredited middleman service like the two listed above, your point rental is fully guaranteed and you don't have to contact anyone besides the professionals at David's or DVC Rental Store. Just be sure to book many months out for the widest selection of accommodations.

## Breaking Down the Discounts

It's tempting to take an all-inclusive approach when booking a Walt Disney World vacation. Disney certainly wants you to adopt a "one-stop shopping" strategy, which is why they offer guests the Magic Your Way package linking resort rooms to theme park tickets. You will also be encouraged to add on the pre-paid Disney Dining Plan, thereby upgrading your booking into a Magic Your Way Plus package.

There may be better ways to book your room and tickets (we'll discuss the Disney Dining Plan in Step Four), particularly since the rules governing a Disney package are stickier than the ones binding you to a "room-only" stay. For example, if you had a sudden emergency in your family, you'd have more wiggle room to cancel a room-only stay in the days leading up to your trip, and be fully refunded your deposit. By booking a package, you'll lose $200 once you pass the 30-day threshold before you check in, and everything within two days of your trip, unless you've purchased travel protection.

So what's the best way to save money with Disney? As with all things, it depends. But you'll almost always save money by booking a room-only discount, unless "free dining" is offered during the length of your onsite stay.

Let's talk about these booking options in more detail.

**ROOM-ONLY DISCOUNT.** Different room discounts are offered throughout the year, saving guests 10–30% off a Disney resort booking (you'll save most on Deluxe accommodations). Be advised—if you tack on tickets to a room-only discount, you'll be purchasing a Magic Your Way package and will be subject to package rules for down payments and cancellation penalties.

You may also find room-only discounts through online travel aggregates like Expedia, Orbitz, CheapTickets, Travelocity, Southwest and Priceline. Make sure you give these sites a try if you're coming up empty for the resort you want with Disney, since these companies typically purchase big blocks of rooms in advance and may yet show openings.

Another benefit of booking a room-only discount is that you're affording yourself greater flexibility in your ticket and dining options by not locking yourself into the kind of vacation Disney thinks you ought to have. Purchasing tickets from a Walt Disney World-authorized vendor will save you money over buying tickets directly from Disney. (See Step Three.)

But here's another thing to consider: my family and I have experimented with the Disney Dining Plan and realized that we'd rather retain the flexibility in eating the way we want to—and not worry about how many snack credits we need to use to "get our money's worth." Sometimes—again, depending on your party's touring and dining preferences—what passes for "convenience" is just another hoop to jump through.

Alternatively, if you like the idea of having a set amount of food available to you each day, and enjoy figuring out how to maximize your dining credits with the entrees you'll order, you may find a lot of value in a Dining Plan.

Your best chance at nabbing a great room-only discount is to travel during the Value season, which starts after New Year's and runs through early February. The next best time? In the fall months, when kids are back in school

**FREE DINING.** This promotion's specifics varies on the year it's being offered, but it is usually available during off-peak weeks in the late summer and fall months, concluding in early December. It normally requires at least a 4-night stay at a Disney resort, and the purchase of a 4-day Park Hopper ticket (thus preventing guests from purchasing discounted tickets from a Walt Disney World-authorized vendor or buying a base ticket, reviewed in the next chapter).

What does "free dining" mean for you and your party? When staying at a Value or Moderate resort, each person

The largest room discounts pop up for Deluxe accommodations, including Disney's Grand Floridian Resort & Spa.

will receive two "quick-service" meals daily, in addition to getting two snack credits and a refillable resort drink mug for the duration of your stay. All of this comes at no additional cost. If you decide to move up a level and book Deluxe, your group members will receive the same benefits but substitute a "table-service" meal at a better restaurant for one of the two quick-service meals. Again—everything is free, except for tips and any extras such as appetizers.

Eating at Walt Disney World is an expensive proposition if you're doing most of your dining at the parks, resorts, and Disney Springs. Nabbing a "free dining" offer is often worth as much as, if not more than, a room-only discount, especially if there are three or more guests staying in a single Disney resort room, or you have young children in your party. However, when staying at a Value or Moderate, it might not be as great a deal for your family, since you'll be confined to eating at quick-service dining locations for every meal. (Alternatively, you may upgrade to the regular Disney Dining Plan. For a family of four, this will cost about a hundred dollars extra per night.)

"Free dining" is Walt Disney World's most popular promotional offer. Just ask any travel agent the week it becomes available: people love the idea of eating for free, even if it doesn't save them much money over a room-only discount. Sometimes, it all comes down to human nature. We all want to feel like we're getting away with something, even if that "something" doesn't save us a huge amount in the long run. We'll talk more "free dining" in Step Four.

Other booking options include:

- **PACKAGE OFFERS.** Disney will offer its guests various package deals depending on the travel season. These offers are generally a room-only discount dressed up in prettier "package" clothing. They're fine to book and will definitely save you money over a Magic Your Way package, but again, you won't usually save more than you would with a room-only discount and will now be bound by Disney package rules for cancellations and payments.

- **TICKETLESS PACKAGES WITH A DINING PLAN.** These are Magic Your Way packages without park tickets, often comparable to room-only discounts, with a full-priced Disney Dining Plan thrown in. Again, package rules apply, though you can still save money over a Magic Your Way package by buying tickets elsewhere.

- **FLORIDA RESIDENT DISCOUNTS.** Florida residents can often find steeper room discounts than the general public, but you must provide proof of residency upon check-in. Good for a last-minute vacation or quick weekend getaway.

- **"ARMED FORCES SALUTE" ROOM DISCOUNTS.** If you're a member of the armed services, but are not staying at Shades of Green (Walt Disney World's low-priced, Deluxe accommodation for military, DoD personnel, and vets), then booking a room using this discount will save you more than publicly available offers. Disney Dining Plans may be added to these phoned-in offers.

- **ANNUAL PASSHOLDER DISCOUNTS.** Not many new Walt Disney World vacationers will spring for an Annual Pass right out of the gate, but if you're anticipating being at Walt Disney World for more than one trip, consider this option for the second stay, as it can secure you a 30% room discount when booking 2–4 months in advance. Annual Passholders also save on dining and merchandise and will receive Memory Maker—Walt Disney World's valuable photo package (a $169 value)—as a pretty substantial perk. Because you don't need to purchase theme park tickets with this discount, it will often work out to your advantage to book a room this way—especially when booking accommodations for a large group. Only one person needs to upgrade to an Annual Pass to secure benefits for the entire travel party. Dining Plans may be purchased, though "free dining" is never offered to Disney's Annual Passholders.

STEP THREE

# Picking the Right Ticket at the Right Price

Now that you've settled on accommodations, it's time to consider which Walt Disney World ticket offers the right blend of affordability and flexibility for your travel party. In this chapter, we'll look at the pros and cons of each ticket "tier" before highlighting some cost-saving strategies.

Any child under three years of age enjoys free admission to all of Walt Disney World's theme parks. This holds true for toddlers turning three while in Orlando. Obviously, this is a huge incentive to plan a family trip before that critical birthday threshold. When staying at a Disney resort, any young child will receive a Magic Band to wear (like big brother or sister) and can come along with the rest of her family on any FastPass+ attraction for which he meets the height requirement (i.e., he does not need a FP+ reservation made for him in your My Disney Experience account).

If you have a child between three and nine years of age at the time of check-in, he will require a child's ticket for the number of days he's visiting Disney's theme parks. You'll find children's tickets to be slightly cheaper than their adult alternative, but you must make FastPass+ reservations through your My Disney Experience account for anyone 3 years and older in your party.

Since you're planning an entire vacation around Walt Disney World, and not just visiting for a day or two, you'll need to purchase multi-day tickets in advance, at a discount. (Oneand two-day tickets may be bought at the gate.) It's essential to know beforehand that all multi-day tickets must be used 4-14 days after their first use, depending on the length of ticket. You cannot purchase a 10-day Base ticket, use five of them during one vacation, and use the remaining five visits on another trip the following year. Nor can you buy tickets for a trip that's two years out, to avoid a rise in prices.

# The Base Ticket

The least expensive Walt Disney World ticket option is the Magic Your Way base ticket, which permits guests to visit one park per day, as many times as they'd like. This ticket is recommended for:

- Families with young children
- Groups who plan on frequenting Disney Springs or other Orlando destinations, making theme park time less of a priority
- Parties visiting during busy weeks of the year, when the extra travel times make park hopping less appealing
- Guests who turn in early in the evenings
- Budget-conscious travelers: the expense of adding a Park Hopper option to a 4-day base ticket costs about $85/adult.

Buying a base ticket is one of the easiest ways to save money on your Walt Disney World vacation. In the past, critics have complained that Disney's Animal Kingdom and Hollywood Studios were "half day parks," making base tickets more limiting to guests on days they visited those destinations, but with the addition of Pandora, Toy Story Land, and Star Wars: Galaxy's Edge in 2017-2019, that critique no longer holds water. Rest assured that if you end up deciding that base tickets are the right choice for your group, you'll still find plenty at the parks to occupy your time, and may even discover a certain level of peace in taking things one day at a time.

# Park Hopper

The next step up is the Magic Your Way base ticket with a Park Hopper option, or, simply, the Park Hopper. This ticket permits guests to visit any of Disney's four theme parks on any day, as many times as they like. Technically, you could start your day at Animal Kingdom in the morning, hop over to Hollywood Studios around lunch, venture to Epcot for dinner, and put a cap on the night by watching the Happily Ever After fireworks show at Magic Kingdom. You'd likely be exhausted, but the advantage of purchasing a Park Hopper ticket is that you have the freedom to do what you want. Here are my recommendations for which Walt Disney World guests should consider buying a Park Hopper ticket before venturing to Orlando:

- People who prize flexibility and spontaneity

- Fans of Disney's nighttime entertainment: every theme park has a not-to-miss nighttime spectacular, and Hollywood Studios has two that can't be watched in the same night, making the ability to hop to a different park in the evening invaluable

- Disney resort guests who plan on using Extra Magic Hours at one park, but would like the ability to "hop" to a different park later since EMH tends to make the parks more crowded

- Guests traveling during less busy times of the year, when transportation between parks and resorts isn't as big of a hassle

- Guests of the three monorail resorts, along with those staying at Fort Wilderness and Wilderness Lodge, since Park Hopper tickets make frequent visits to Magic Kingdom easier

- Guests of an Epcot resort (Yacht Club, Beach Club, BoardWalk, or Swan & Dolphin) will also appreciate the ability to hop to Epcot at their convenience, especially during festival times

- Parties with a lot of advance dining reservations, particularly if those ADRs are scattered throughout the parks

My family park hops because we enjoy the flexibility of spending our mornings in one park, and then heading back to our resort for a mid-day break before later exploring a different park's evening entertainment. These tickets allow for more flexibility in a place that otherwise demands stringent planning, and that's refreshing—even to this micro-manager.

One of the great benefits of having a Park Hopper is the ability to hop to Magic Kingdom later in the day. Not only can you enjoy that park's extended hours, but you can also take advantage of the fact that there is typically more FastPass+ availability at Magic Kingdom, since more rides offer it. We'll delve into this more thoroughly in Step Seven, but guests can often nab a 4th, 5th, and even 6th FP+ selection at Magic Kingdom.

# Park Hopper Plus

The Park Hopper Plus ticket is the best value for your vacation dollar, and my family's go-to ticket on every Orlando trip. Not only can you tour as many parks as you like on any given day with a Park Hopper Plus, you also have access to Disney's two wonderfully themed water parks—Typhoon Lagoon and Blizzard Beach—in addition to ESPN Wide World of Sports, the Oak Trail Golf Course, and two miniature golf courses.

How does it work? Let's say you've bought a 5-day Park Hopper Plus ticket. In addition to having unlimited entry into Disney's four main theme parks for five days, you may also visit five of the destinations listed above, either on the same days you visit Magic Kingdom, Animal Kingdom, Hollywood Studios, and Epcot, or on "down" days designed for greater relaxation. So, with the purchase of a 5-day Park Hopper Plus ticket, you potentially have 9 days of Disney entertainment, when spreading out destination visits. (5-day tickets expire within 9 days.) The five extra visits could be distributed among the six destinations any way you like—if you're a water park person, and want to spend four days at Typhoon Lagoon and one day at Blizzard Beach, that's your privilege. Within the waterparks, guests enjoy all-day access for the "price" of a single visit. (For golf, one visit = one round.) And at $21 extra/person above the price of a regular Park Hopper, all you need is one waterpark visit to make this ticket a slam-dunk investment.

If you found the arguments for the Park Hopper ticket compelling, and fall into one of the categories below, consider buying a Park Hopper Plus:

A Park Hopper Plus ticket grants its owner admission to Typhoon Lagoon, one of two Walt Disney World water parks.

- Planning on visiting a water park (not as likely in the winter)
- Have a long enough trip planned that extra destinations sound appealing

## Annual Pass

The notion of buying an Annual Pass, which grants the passholder year-round privileges to Walt Disney World's four theme parks (and two water parks, if you purchase the Platinum Plus), might seem an odd proposition for a first-time visitor. Considering the expense of an Annual Pass ($1,119 in 2020 for the "standard" Platinum version), it's not likely to behoove many Disney vacationers to make this kind of investment up front. But there are a few instances when it might be worth your while, because of the special benefits accorded to passholders, such as:

- Free theme park parking, a boon to non-Disney resort guests
- 10-20% dining discounts at select restaurants
- 20% merchandise discount at select locations

- 15% off select tours and experiences
- Complimentary PhotoPass downloads; this is like getting Memory Maker, discussed in Step Nine, for free, which not only benefits the passholder, but also her friends and family
- Spa, golfing, and boat rental discounts
- Larger room discounts, though Annual Passholder discounts are offered later than most

Although you're not likely to purchase an Annual Pass for your first trip to Orlando, it's worth considering if planning a longer trip with a large party, if you'll definitely be purchasing Memory Maker, have lots of ADRs at restaurants for which the discounts could quickly stack up, or are planning on booking special tours/experiences that will compensate for a larger up-front cost. And certainly, if you can already foresee taking two or three trips within a twelve month period, an Annual Pass is well worth having.

# Upgrading Magic Your Way Tickets

It's reassuring to know that upon arrival at Walt Disney World, you can upgrade your Magic Your Way ticket any way you like, as long as you're within the ticket's expiration window, have at least one unused day of admission left on your ticket (i.e., you can add a fourth day while on the third day of a 3-day ticket), and are not trying to add days beyond the 10-day maximum visit length (in which case you'd upgrade to an Annual Pass). Just visit any Guest Relations window inside or outside the four major theme parks, the two water parks, or at the Disney Springs Ticket Center. You may not upgrade tickets via email or phone.

The freedom to upgrade is beneficial to visitors deciding, while already in Orlando, that they want to tack on another day of Disney fun to their vacations, or for those who regret not taking advantage of the Park Hopper's greater flexibility. An upgrade might be in store for those who decide the weather is nice enough to explore the water parks (making the Park Hopper Plus a necessity) or for those guests who fall in love with the parks and want to arrange another trip soon, making the Annual Pass worthwhile. What's important to know is that even while upgrading, you keep the discount secured by buying your ticket online in advance. In other words, Disney reads the cost of your original ticket as their "gate price," and only charges you for the amount above that number for the new, upgraded ticket. You will not lose out by buying your tickets ahead of time, even if you decide that ticket needs upgrading later on.

I recommend photographing the back of your tickets and sending those pics to yourself via email, just in case your tickets (and/or your camera) are lost or stolen. Having those ticket ID numbers can be a lifesaver when it comes to Disney reissuing lost ones. Alternatively, you can link the tickets immediately to your My Disney Experience account and avoid the worry altogether.

## Where to Buy

It's essential to buy your Walt Disney World tickets far enough in advance to link them to your My Disney Experience account, so you can start making FP+ reservations before visiting the theme parks. For Disney resort guests, this means buying ahead of the 60-day reservation window. For offsite guests, you'll want tickets linked up 30 days prior to your arrival.

It's in your financial interest to buy your ticket from an authorized online Disney ticket broker, unless you can get a military discount, or are a Florida resident, in which case you'd purchase directly from Disney. Never buy tickets off eBay or Craigslist or from anyone promising a deal that seems too good to be true. It likely is

Although AAA does offer discounted Walt Disney World tickets, their rates are not typically as good as the brokers listed below:

- **PARK SAVERS.** I find that Park Savers consistently offers good deals, but you have to be comfortable receiving a voucher by email, instead of a paper ticket that's mailed to you. Once you receive your ticket confirmation numbers, assign them to each member of your party in your My Disney Experience account (discussed in

Step Six). If you have a MagicBand, there is no need to print out the vouchers and take them to a park ticket window to be granted admission into the parks. Without a MagicBand, you must take this additional step for any initial theme park entry.

- **UNDERCOVER TOURIST.** A trusted, experienced name when it comes to theme park touring. Undercover Tourist will mail your tickets via USPS, which you can photograph before linking the ticket ID numbers to your MDE account. They can also send them via email, depending on your preferences. These folks have been around for a while and pride themselves on their excellent customer service. In fact, their entire website provides invaluable information for anyone heading to Orlando's theme parks.

STEP FOUR

# Deciding on the Dining Plan

There are two factors to consider when deciding whether to purchase a Disney Dining Plan to cover the cost of your vacation meals: value and convenience. In this chapter, we'll discuss how the Dining Plan affects your vacation expenses and whether the "all-inclusive" benefits Disney advertises are worth the added cost.

First, though, it's important to understand that Disney only offers its Dining Plans to guests staying at a Walt Disney World resort (not including Shades of Green, or the Swan and Dolphin). Guests renting points from Disney Vacation Club members may also add a Dining Plan to their room reservation, without purchasing tickets, if they book the plan at least 48 hours in advance of their arrival. If you've booked a hotel, condo, or vacation home offsite of Disney property, you may not purchase a Disney Dining Plan and can move onto Step Five without a backward glance.

You may add a Dining Plan to a room-only reservation, making your stay a "ticketless package" in Disney parlance. To do this, you must either a) call 407-W-DISNEY and ask the helpful cast member to do it for you or b) use a travel agent. You may not buy a ticketless package online. Also: you cannot receive the "free dining" promotion when purchasing a ticketless package—you must buy your tickets from Disney if "free dining" is offered during your trip dates.

There are three types of Disney Dining Plan. Before diving into their details, let's first unravel some Disney dining terminology:

- **QUICK-SERVICE MEAL.** A meal that includes an entree, side item, and drink at a Disney counter-service restaurant. Roughly equivalent to a fast food or food court meal. Disney allows guests to substitute "specialty" drinks (including smoothies, hot chocolate, and milkshakes) or alcoholic beverages for soda or water, where available.

- **TABLE-SERVICE MEAL.** A meal that includes an entree, dessert, and beverage at a nicer restaurant in which your food is brought to the table. Buffets are included. Again, you may substitute a specialty drink or alcoholic beverage for a regular drink where available. You may also substitute a side item (soup, salad, fruit) for dessert. Table-service restaurants normally require ADRs (advance dining reservations).

- **SNACK.** A snack encompasses a wide variety of single-service items found throughout the parks, from food and beverages sold at snack carts to desserts and side items that may be ordered specially at festival food booths and counter-service restaurants. Look for the purple and white DDP symbol for guidance.

Disney's Dining Plans are pooled into either quick-service, table-service, or snack "credits," depending on which type of plan is purchased, and are allocated for the number of nights you're staying on Disney property. (If you're there 4 nights, but will be in the parks for 5 days, you'll have to apportion your credits accordingly, and pay out of pocket for food purchased once your credits are gone.) When going to "pay" for a meal, the Disney cast member will scan your MagicBand or ticket, and see how many pooled credits remain on your party's dining balance, deducting the number required for that meal. Remaining Dining Plan credits will appear at the bottom of your receipt, and in the My Disney Experience app.

Credits can be "spent" any way you like during your stay—in other words, you don't have a certain quota to spend per day, but an allowance for your party throughout a vacation. Cast members will ensure you have the correct number of side items, beverages, and/or desserts permitted to you. When you've ordered more than your share, you'll pay for extra items out of pocket. This is important: tips are not included in the Dining Plan. If eating at a table-service restaurant, you should definitely leave your server a tip! If there are six or more in your party, an 18% gratuity will be added to the bill.

Now let's get to the plans themselves.

# Disney Quick-Service Dining Plan

This plan includes:

- 2 quick-service meals per person, per night of your stay
- 2 snacks per person, per night
- 1 drink mug per person, for all fountain drink, tea, or coffee refills at your resort's quick-service restaurant

In 2019, the Quick-Service Dining Plan cost $55 per adult per night, and $26 per child per night. Note that you may not use this Dining Plan at any of Disney's table-service or signature (fine dining) restaurants. The one exception is Be Our Guest in Magic Kingdom, which offers breakfast and lunch entrees for one quick-service dining credit.

# Disney Dining Plan

This plan includes:

- 1 quick-service meal per person, per night
- 1 table-service meal per person, per night
- 2 snacks per person, per night
- 1 drink mug per person, for all fountain drink, tea, or coffee refills at your resort's quick-service restaurant

In 2019, the Disney Dining Plan cost $78 per adult per night, and $30.50 per child per night.

# Disney Deluxe Dining Plan

This plan includes:

- 3 meal credits per person, per night, to be used at any quick-service, table-service, or "signature" restaurant
- 2 snacks per person, per night

- 1 drink mug per person, for all fountain drink, tea, or coffee refills at your resort's quick-service restaurant

In 2020, the Deluxe Dining Plan cost $119 per adult per night, and $47.50 per child per night.

If it's difficult for you to imagine eating three table-service meals per day, and still being able to walk by the end of the night, I share your concern. However, many guests purchasing the Deluxe Dining Plan will adopt a different strategy: eating one table-service meal for breakfast or lunch, and one "signature" meal for dinner. Disney's finest restaurants, and its dinner shows, cost two table-service credits per meal. These are special dining experiences deserving of your notice, but be forewarned: eating at a signature restaurant is not normally two times as expensive as eating at a table-service restaurant. It's more like one-and-a-half. For the average Disney guest, the Deluxe Dining Plan, used in a typical fashion, is not a good value. And never use a Deluxe Dining credit for a counter-service meal. That's definitely a waste of money.

Guests can make an advance dining reservation at Via Napoli, the Epcot ristorante renowned for its delicious wood-fired pizza.

Each person listed on your Walt Disney World resort reservation must purchase the same Dining Plan. Children under three are not permitted on a Dining Plan, but may share your restaurant meal, and will receive their own plate at any Disney buffet (drink included). Children 3–9 must order off the child's menu, unless they're on the Quick-Service Dining Plan, in which case they may order an adult entree. (Disney doesn't track adult vs. child quick-service dining credits.) Because Disney is so accommodating of guests' wishes, it's often possible to order a "child-sized" portion of a regular-menu entree when dining at table-service restaurants. So if you have a special request—just ask! Your server will let you know what she can do for you.

If you're going to Epcot for a festival, you can use one quick-service meal credit to purchase three snacks offered at any of the outdoor kitchen booths. It's easy to buy an entire meal's worth of food in this manner, and festival "snacks" are often more interesting than what you'd find at most counter-service restaurants. Alternatively, you can use your snack credits to purchase festival food. Disney Dining Plan guests often find that they don't need two snacks per day, so this is an excellent way of "spending" leftover credits, since festival snacks are pricier.

## Should You Buy a Dining Plan?

It depends. By and large, though, I think most guests should not purchase a Dining Plan when vacationing at Walt Disney World, unless they're offered the free dining promotion. Here are the reasons why:

- Most people will spend less money out of pocket than on any of Disney's Dining Plans. In order to make the Dining Plan work for you, guests must commit themselves to buying the more expensive menu items. This is especially difficult for vegetarians and fans of chicken and pasta. If you're a devoted eater of steak and lobster, though, you can get your money's worth! For everyone else, it's unlikely. Which leads me to the next point...

- This is a lot of food. Don't get me wrong: I look forward to our Disney vacations partly because I let myself eat what I want. When you're on vacation, rules of restraint should be relaxed. But often, when on the Dining Plan, I feel like I must eat in order to get my money's worth. Do I really need a milkshake at 11:30 in the morning with lunch? Probably not, if I'm planning on having a snack in a few hours, and a dessert with dinner. When you're on a Disney Dining Plan, you tend to overdo it...because you've already paid for it. This is especially true of the Deluxe Dining Plan.

- When on the Dining Plan or Deluxe Dining Plan, you commit yourself to a large number of table-service meals requiring ADRs. This eats up vacation time. I think some of those hours—especially for first-time guests—are better spent experiencing the parks (especially if you have young children who will balk at sitting still in nicer restaurants). By all means, make some ADRs! I love Disney food and the time I've spent with my family enjoying Disney's restaurants. But keep in mind that you're committing yourself to being in a certain spot, at an appointed hour, on a specific day, and cannot break that ADR at short notice unless you cough up a $10/person cancellation fee. Purchasing a Dining Plan makes a Disney vacation less flexible and accommodating, unless you're on the Quick-Service Plan.

- This point ties into the last one: planning out so many ADRs, and learning how best to maximize your dining credits, consumes pre-trip time as well. For some people, this is part of the fun of planning a Walt Disney World vacation. To others, the idea of scrutinizing the prices of entrees they'll be eating six months from now seems a little nuts.

That being said, a lot of Disney fans love using the Dining Plan, and they are popular with onsite guests, mainly because they offer the feel of an all-inclusive vacation, similar to what you'd get on a cruise. There is a built-in, psychological relief to the Dining Plan that Disney exploits well, and I'm not immune to its charms. When you've already paid for something, the stress of nickel-and-diming everything seems to be magically allayed. For example, if your son desperately wants a cinnamon roll from Gaston's Tavern during an early morning Magic Kingdom visit, and you see it's a snack by Disney Dining standards, you may be inclined to get it for him. After all, it's been paid for! Whereas, if you were forced to take that extra step of pulling the four dollars from your pocket, you might refuse, especially if he'd already eaten breakfast that morning. In this way, a Disney Dining Plan allows you to spoil your kids a little, which isn't a bad thing.

The single best way to save money on your food expenditures at Walt Disney World is to eat breakfast in your room. If you have a rental car, that means picking up some groceries on the way to your hotel. When reliant on Disney transportation, look into having groceries delivered via Amazon Prime Now or Garden Grocer (Disney charges a $6 fee for deliveries). If you are on a Disney Dining Plan, try not to use your meal credits for morning meals—unless it's a pricey character breakfast or a quick-service credit at Be Our Guest. And if you have to hit your resort food court in the morning, search out those items that can be bought with a snack credit, like muffins and bagels with cream cheese, in lieu of wasting a dining credit on a less important meal.

While I understand the perceived convenience a Disney Dining Plan offers guests, I'd like to suggest an alternative: figure out a dining budget ahead of your trip, and stick to it by using Disney gift cards you've purchased in advance. Gift cards can often be bought with accompanying "fuel point" savings at grocery stores and warehouse clubs, or can help earn you points via your credit card rewards program.

In this way, you can still enjoy a bit of that "all inclusive" feel to your vacation, while spending less than you might with a Dining Plan. Of course, you can do the same thing without using gift cards. Just keep track of your receipts each day, and note where you stand with regard to your allowance. Think about what you'll spend at any "splurge" restaurants to come and how you can tighten your purse strings for other, less important meals. This might mean splitting more generous food portions among family members or ordering water instead of soda. When I'm worried about the price of a meal, that overpriced drink is the first thing to go. I also take care to look at the children's menu at many counter-service restaurants, since adults are free to order these items, and a child's entree is often plenty filling for people with smaller appetites. Make sure you've factored in one delicious treat per day for everyone, though, so nobody leaves the park feeling deprived. Just make it later in the day, so that when you have to refuse your child a Mickey ice cream bar, or that cinnamon roll, in the early hours, you can assure them there are better things yet to come.

## Exceptions

There are Disney guests for whom the Dining Plan is a sensible, cost-saving measure, and I don't want to overlook them. Walt Disney World offers a number of character meals at special restaurants, in which guests can eat while interacting with beloved Disney characters, posing for photos and getting autographs between bites of food. These are among the most popular experiences on Disney property. If you have children for whom you want to book a lot of character meals at fun, but pricey, destinations like Chef Mickey's, Akershus Royal Banquet Hall, or 'Ohana, then buying the regular Disney Dining Plan will save you money. Likewise, if you're set on purchasing Disney dining packages for shows like Fantasmic! at Hollywood Studios, or Rivers of Light at Animal Kingdom, you can maximize the value of a table-service dining credit when applying them toward these special dining events. (Dining packages come with preferential seating for Disney shows, eliminating the need to spend a FastPass+ reservation on similar access.)

With the recent addition of alcoholic beverages to Disney's dining credits, the Dining Plans may also be a better value for guests who regularly enjoy an adult beverage with their meals. (Not every restaurant will serve alcohol, though.) The ability to substitute a specialized beverage such as a milkshake or smoothie is appealing to kids and adults who want a dessert but might not otherwise spring for one. In this way, the value of the Dining Plan rose significantly in the last two years.

# What about "Free Dining?"

Each spring, usually in April or May, Disney releases "free dining" dates for guests booking rooms at select Walt Disney World resorts. These dates, during which guests receive either the Quick-Service Dining Plan or regular Dining Plan for "free" with their package reservation, historically fall during less crowded weeks in late summer and autumn, stopping just shy of the holiday season. Free Dining is Disney's most popular promotion, in part because our brains are configured to light up whenever we hear the word "free." Just remember that you're paying full price for a room when accepting this promotion in lieu of another discount. Disney's Free Dining offer also requires the purchase of, at minimum, a 4or 5-day Park Hopper ticket for everyone in your party. (If you planned on purchasing a base ticket, this substitution will squeeze your budget. It also deprives you of savings you'd see by buying your tickets from authorized ticket brokers.) Look for the date you'll arrive at Walt Disney World to see if it's eligible for Free Dining. You may still qualify if you arrive just prior to a blackout's start.

Should you take Free Dining over a room or package discount? Here's where I come down on this: if you are a family of three or more people staying in a single room at a Value or Moderate resort, Free Dining can probably save you money over a stand-alone room discount. It's not as slam-dunk of a case as it used to be, however, due to the distressing fact that, in its present incarnation, guests staying at a Moderate resort no longer receive the regular Dining Plan with their Disney packages, but are offered the Quick-Service Plan instead. This represents a substantial loss of value from prior years, since Moderate resort guests can no longer make ADRs at Disney's popular buffets, character meals, and other table-service restaurants. You may upgrade the Quick-Service Dining Plan to Disney's standard Dining Plan, but that's pulling more money from your pocket. When staying Deluxe, I'd stick with the meatier room discount Disney usually offers its Deluxe guests, and only consider Free Dining if there were four of us in a single room, and we had settled on a less expensive Deluxe resort.

My biggest piece of advice about Free Dining is to check the room discounts being offered on your travel dates, and see if the savings per night will amount to more than what you'd spend on food per day for everyone in your room. If you need to look up current food prices at Walt Disney World, every restaurant's menu can be found on Disney's website.

# Choosing Transportation That Works for You

From its four theme parks to its two water parks and twenty-five resorts, Walt Disney World encompasses a sprawling network of highways, roads, and waterways, all of which must be negotiated by guests who are often unfamiliar with its scope and layout. To save yourself time and needless headaches, then, it's a smart idea to consider well in advance of your trip the best strategies for getting around.

**OFFSITE GUESTS.** It's simple: if you're flying into Orlando, you'll want to rent a car at the Orlando International Airport. While it's possible to use a taxi, Uber, or Lyft to get to your hotel from the airport, and then to rely on your hotel's theme park shuttles to transport you around Walt Disney World, I can't recommend this strategy, due to the rather rigid timetables—and crowded vehicles—most hotels offer as an alternative to Disney transportation. You'll be happier having your own car.

Offsite guests must pay $25 to park at any of the four theme parks. If you hop to a different park later in the day, you won't have to pay again, as long as you keep your receipt. It's free to park at Blizzard Beach and Typhoon Lagoon, and at Disney's two miniature golf courses. As an offsite guest, you may still use Disney boats, buses, Skyliner and monorail service wherever convenient. Magic Kingdom and Epcot are connected via monorail, so it may make sense to park at one theme park or the other when visiting both in the same day. As we'll see later on, getting from the Magic Kingdom parking lot through that park's front gate is the most complicated, and time-consuming, procedure in all of Walt Disney World. Once you're there, however, it's easy enough to visit all the resorts—and their restaurants—on the monorail loop, so that even offsite guests may find themselves enjoying quality time on Disney transportation. For visits to Animal Kingdom, guests will need to use a bus or car. Disney's Hollywood Studios is accessible by bus or car, foot or Friendship boat (from Epcot and the Epcot-area resorts), or the new Skyliner gondola system, the aerial artery connecting Epcot and Hollywood Studios, making stops at four Disney resorts.

**ONSITE GUESTS.** The transportation choice is tougher here. Should you rent a car while staying onsite or rely exclusively on Disney transportation throughout your vacation? Let's break down the options to simplify your decision.

A rental car would be beneficial for:

- Independent drivers comfortable navigating a car with the help of GPS or smartphone assistance
- Introverts needing a people break
- Impatient folks who don't like waiting around for a bus
- Guests who plan on visiting other Orlando destinations throughout their stay
- Guests who plan on visiting a number of Disney resorts

Rental cars are likely not necessary for:

- Budget-conscious travelers who don't want to pay for a car along with Disney's resort parking fees; rentals requiring car seats will be an added expense
- Laid back, go-with-the-flow vacationers
- Guests staying in close proximity to Magic Kingdom or Epcot
- People who are comfortable using taxi or rideshare services, or the new Minnie vans that Disney rolled out to its onsite guests for travels within Walt Disney World

Here are some tips for saving money on your Orlando car rental:

- Check autoslash.com for the latest drops in car prices

- Join a car rental loyalty program to receive free upgrades and streamline the rental process
- If possible, play around with pick-up and drop-off times to cut a day off your rental rate
- Refuse insurance if your auto policy covers car rentals
- Fill up the tank before returning your car instead of paying the rental company's excessive charge

Be aware that there are toll roads connecting Orlando to Walt Disney World. You can pay cash for these tolls, instead of purchasing a Sun Pass or other toll-service package the rental car service is peddling. You must pay all tolls, however, or face a hefty charge once you get back home.

Hopefully, you have a feel for what kind of transportation works best for you. Our family has tried it both ways, and we now rent a car on every Disney trip. We like the freedom of being able to get around on our own terms, and I have no qualms about driving in unfamiliar territory, as long as I have my smartphone dictating directions at me. Your family might feel differently. If you have young children requiring car seats, that's another factor to consider. I have seen kids in strollers conk out without a problem on the monorail and Disney buses, working in a nap when they needed rest most. Some vacationers genuinely enjoy striking up conversations with their fellow travelers on the various Disney vehicles, while older kids might view a boat or monorail ride with the same giddy enthusiasm they reserve for other Disney attractions. To some degree, being "stuck" with Disney transportation is really what you make of it. Yes, it might take longer to get around. That doesn't mean it's "wasted" time. It really comes down to expectations.

For people using Disney transportation exclusively, and for offsite guests who will utilize the monorail and/or ferry system to get to Magic Kingdom, the information that follows is crucial to seeing you through every leg of your Walt Disney World journey.

**MAGICAL EXPRESS.** Walt Disney World provides complimentary bus transportation from the Orlando International Airport to its resorts for guests who've booked the service in advance, either by selecting "ground transportation" in their My Disney Experience account or by calling 866-599-0951 (U.S.) and speaking with a Disney cast member. Resort guests using Disney's Magical Express will receive luggage tags prior to their trip, so that Disney can pick up your bags at the airport and deliver them to your room shortly after your arrival. (This is true for flights arriving up to 10 p.m. If you arrive between 10:00 p.m. and 5:00 a.m., you will have to pick up your bags from the carousel yourself.) After disembarking in Orlando, make your way to the airport's ground floor, where you will see signage directing you toward Magical Express. Once there, you'll seldom wait more than 30 minutes to board a bus and be on your way.

Riding Magical Express can serve as the perfect segue into a Disney vacation. Kids will enjoy the familiar characters in the introductory video that plays on the way to your resort, while adults will appreciate the useful information therein.

That said, it may take more time than you think to get to your resort, depending on the order in which the Magical Express' other guests are dropped off. Also, when it comes time to depart your resort at the end of your vacation, the Magical Express will pick you up a full three hours before your flight's departure (four hours for international flights). This makes for an awfully early morning for some travelers.

On the morning of your departure to the Orlando airport, think about using your resort's airport check-in service to secure your boarding pass and check your bags. You may only do this from 5:00 a.m. to noon, but it will save you time at the airport later.

**DISNEY BUSES.** While Walt Disney World offers monorail, boat, gondola, and Minnie van transportation service, most onsite guests will spend the bulk of their travel time aboard one of Disney's 350+ buses.

Resort buses start running around 6:30am to Magic Kingdom (and earlier if the park opens at 7:00 or 8:00), and around 7:00 to the other theme parks, so that guests with pre-park-opening breakfast reservations can get to their restaurants on time. Buses for the various theme parks and Disney Springs pull up every twenty minutes, on average, though the schedule varies according to the time of day (buses arrive most frequently in the mornings). You may encounter a freak occurrence or two, in which you'll have to wait for a bus in excess of 40 minutes, but this is becoming an increasingly rare phenomenon. Disney installed new screens at their resorts' bus depots apprising guests of the next arrival, in addition to providing updates via the MDE app. When a bus pulls up, guests in wheelchairs or motorized scooters will embark first. Strollers are permitted, but you should fold them before boarding. Buses can be crowded during early morning and late night hours, and some guests may have to stand. Several Disney resorts share bus lines, which can add extra minutes to your travel time.

When leaving a theme park to return to your resort, or to travel to a different Disney World destination, follow the signs to the appropriate bus depot, and wait there. You may catch buses from the theme parks to Disney Springs from 4:00–11:00pm, and from your resorts to the water parks, though these pass by less frequently. Whatever your destination, it's imperative that you leave yourself plenty of time to traverse the massive Walt Disney World resort. This is especially true when traveling to an ADR (advance dining reservation). Grant yourself an hour to make the jaunt between theme parks, or for the journey from your resort to a theme park's front gates. Allot 90 minutes when traveling to a resort ADR, since you'll have to take the bus to that resort's most proximal theme park, before boarding a bus to the resort itself. All this takes time! There are no buses that run between resorts (unless you share a bus line with that resort). Negotiating ADRs is one of the biggest reasons Uber and Lyft have become so popular with Disney World guests in recent years.

Buses run for about an hour after each theme park's closing. So you might not want to make a mad dash for the gates after the last firework trail fades from the night sky. Instead, take some time to walk around and enjoy the parks at night or do some shopping. By the time you make your way leisurely out of the park, the worst of the crowds will have dissipated, and you can board a bus more freely.

Even if you've rented a car while staying on Disney property, take your resort's bus to Magic Kingdom. While it's faster to drive to every other Disney destination, Magic Kingdom is best negotiated by bus.

**MONORAIL.** Most Disney guests await the arrival of their first monorail ride with as much enthusiasm as that first trip on Space Mountain. This isn't by accident. Walt Disney World's original planners designed the monorail system to serve as the gateway between the real world and the enchanting escape Magic Kingdom promises. The Seven Seas Lagoon was constructed to serve as a water feature separating the park from its parking lot, so that guests would have to leave their cars behind at the Transportation & Ticket Center (TTC) in order to board the monorail and be whisked away to Neverland.

Riding the monorail is an experience utterly unique to Disney. If you're lucky enough to stay at the Contemporary, you'll love watching the monorail pass through its lobby. For guests staying at the Polynesian, Contemporary, or Grand Floridian resorts, the appeal and convenience is unmatched. There's a reason these hotels are known as "the monorail resorts," and why their rooms come at such a steep cost.

There are downsides to the monorail's implementation, however, which are: 1) the creation of another, time-consuming step for entering the extremely popular Magic Kingdom, and 2) the existence of three different monorail lines, which can be confusing to guests.

In negotiating the first obstacle, be sure to give yourself enough time when traveling to Magic Kingdom by car. Magic Kingdom's parking lot is immense, but there are regular trams taking guests up to the TTC, where you will then wait for one of two monorails to Magic Kingdom: the express line, which travels solely between Magic Kingdom and the TTC, or the resort monorail line, which makes five stops: the TTC, the Polynesian, the Grand Floridian, Magic Kingdom, and the Contemporary, before returning to the TTC.

Normally, you'll want to board the express monorail at the TTC, since this is the most efficient route to Magic Kingdom. Exceptions include: 1) you're going to visit a monorail resort, 2) you have an ADR at a monorail resort or a pre-park-opening ADR at Magic Kingdom, or 3) you arrive so early at the TTC that the express line isn't running yet. The resort line opens at 7am most mornings. The express line won't start for an hour or so after that.

The third monorail line is the Epcot line from the TTC to Epcot. If you want to take the monorail from Magic Kingdom to Epcot, or the other way around, you need to disembark at the TTC and board a different monorail there. For that reason, it can sometimes be more efficient to take a bus (if not as much fun).

**FERRIES AND BOATS.** There are three ferries shuttling guests between the TTC and Magic Kingdom, launching from the TTC dock about 45 minutes prior to park opening and taking their last excursion roughly an hour after park closing. This Seven Seas Lagoon cruise lasts 10–12 minutes, and can be just as timely as a monorail ride, depending on your luck. Our family will often take the monorail to the park in the morning and return by ferry later in the day. It's a serene, relaxing wrap-up to a hectic day of Magic Kingdom touring and affords some beautiful vistas of Cinderella Castle and the three monorail

Disney's monorail transports visitors to Epcot,
in addition to Magic Kingdom.

resorts. If you're a photographer, you'll want to take advantage of this opportunity to snap some pics.

The Magic Kingdom resorts also use water transportation to ferry guests back and forth to the park. The boats to and from the Grand Floridian, Polynesian, Contemporary, Wilderness Lodge, and Fort Wilderness resorts generally depart every 20 minutes in both directions. Check the individual boat schedules for starting and stopping times if staying at one of these resorts. Boats are an excellent way of getting to Wilderness Lodge or Fort Wilderness from Magic Kingdom when you have an ADR at one of their restaurants, or simply want to explore the grounds. Friendship boats connect the waterway from Epcot to Hollywood Studios, making stops at the Swan and Dolphin resorts, Yacht and Beach Club resorts, and BoardWalk Inn. This is a leisurely boat ride that is more relaxing than timely, but it is a nice way of breaking up a busy day spent visiting both theme parks. You may also walk between Epcot and Hollywood Studios, which will take you half the time it takes by water: about 20 minutes.

Walking the loop around Epcot's World Showcase can itself be tiring, especially on hot days, so you might find it more convenient to board a Friendship boat within the park as well, which will carry you either between Canada and Morocco, or between Mexico and Germany.

Finally, if you are staying as a guest of Saratoga Springs, Old Key West, Port Orleans Riverside or Port Orleans French Quarter, you'll enjoy the convenience of the Sassagoula River water taxis zipping you over to Disney Springs. These boats stop at the various resorts every 20 minutes, beginning service at 11:00am daily.

**SKYLINER.** Starting in the fall of 2019, Disney guests may travel via aerial gondolas between Epcot and Disney's Hollywood Studios, with additional stops at four onsite resorts: Disney's Riviera Resort (opening in December 2019), Caribbean Beach Resort, and a shared station for guests of Disney's Pop Century Resort and Art of Animation Resorts. Each whimsical, Disney-themed cabin is equipped with bench seating for 10 passengers, and is well-ventilated for the Florida weather, whisking guests through the air at a serene 11 mph to enjoy spectacular views of the parks and resorts in 5-20 minute journeys. Caribbean Beach serves as a primary hub between Epcot and the Studios for guests needing to disembark for alternative Skyliner routing. Travelers in wheelchairs and ECVs, who may require more time for boarding, enjoy separate queues for embarkation. Children may sit in strollers throughout their "flight." In inclement weather, Disney's Skyliner service is halted, and guests should utilize bus or other modes of transportation.

**TAXIS AND RIDESHARE SERVICES.** Occasionally, you won't have the time—or the patience—to navigate the ins and outs of Walt Disney World transportation. This is especially true when traveling between resorts. When you're hard-pressed to make an ADR, or are dangerously close to missing a nightly fireworks show, stay calm. Call up the Uber or Lyft app on your smartphone to request a ride. On the screen, you'll see which driver has received your request and how far away he is from your designated meeting spot. Rideshare vehicles can also be helpful when visiting a nonDisney Orlando destination. At $10–$12 a ride, they make a lot of financial sense, especially for large parties. But if you look more favorably on taxi transportation, those are plentiful, too. There is no rideshare or taxi drop-off point at the Magic Kingdom entrance. If you need a ride to or from that theme park, ask your driver to drop you off, or pick you up, at the nearby Contemporary Resort. Alternatively, you can be dropped off at the Transportation & Ticket Center. Not to be outdone, Disney has partnered with Lyft to roll out their own rideshare vehicles in the form of Minnie vans, now operating at all Disney resorts. The cost for a one-way trip for 1-6 people is $15 + a mileage-based fee, for an average around $33, with special accommodations for guests with disabilities and the included convenience of two car seats. Guests use the Lyft app to call for the nearest Minnie van.

When thinking about using alternative means of transportation, it's important to remember the old adage: time is money. Nowhere is this truer than at Walt Disney World. If you're sweating over how to get from Point A to Point B in the least amount of time, the recent influx of rideshare services around Disney property can seem like a godsend.

**ECV AND WHEELCHAIR RENTALS.** For guests requiring assistance with renting wheelchair or electric convenience vehicles while touring Walt Disney World, consider these options:

- Bring your own wheelchair or ECV, as long as it's within the 32" x 48" size limit.
- Rent one from Disney at a theme park or at Disney Springs.
- Rent one from an outside vendor, which can be dropped off and picked up from your resort at a pre-arranged time.

The benefits of using your own vehicle, or renting one from an outside vendor, come in the money you'll save and the ability to enjoy use of the vehicle at your resort and other non-Disney destinations. The main plus in renting from Disney is the freedom from worrying about getting the wheelchair or ECV into, and out of, Disney's transportation vehicles. Disney's daily rentals cover its use throughout any parks you visit that day. Alternatively, to save money, guests may pay for a length-of-stay wheelchair rental in advance. Note that this does not hold true for ECVs, which are offered as day rentals only. All rentals are on a first-come, first-served basis for Disney guests.

**STROLLER RENTALS.** A Walt Disney World vacation requires a lot of walking, making strollers a prerequisite for parents with young children. As with ECVs and wheelchairs, parents are faced with several choices when it comes to using strollers at Disney World:

- Bring a stroller from home. This makes the most sense when using an "umbrella stroller," which easily can be stowed on airplanes and buses.
- Purchase a cheap stroller in Orlando. Doing so can save you money over renting one. Strollers will be cheaper offsite, but can be bought from Disney's gift shops.
- Rent a single- or double-stroller from Disney, either at a daily rate or a length-of-stay rate, at any theme park or at Disney Springs.
- Rent a less expensive stroller from a trusted outside vendor in advance of your trip, to be delivered to your hotel or resort upon arrival.

# Using the MyDisneyExperience Website and App

Your trip to Walt Disney World is starting to take shape! Now it's time to make those plans official by entering your vacation details into Disney's personalized website: My Disney Experience (MDE). This online vacation planning tool, in conjunction with Disney's mobile app of the same name, will help you organize all your vacation plans in one convenient place, while enabling you to make dining and FastPass+ reservations in advance of your stay. But it doesn't end there. After finalizing your itinerary at home, you can use the MDE app during your Disney World visit to alter any plans as needed, in addition to accessing Disney's theme park maps, attraction wait times, entertainment schedules, character greeting locations, and a plethora of other handy references, all designed to keep your vacation running smoothly.

## Getting to Know MDE

First things first: let's get you signed up for a My Disney Experience account. On your laptop or home computer, go to StartYourDisneyExperience.com and create an account by choosing a login ID and password. Then download the free My Disney Experience (MDE) app to your tablet, iPhone, or android device. Your login information is the same across all platforms.

I find it easier to link my reservations on the website, but you can use the app as well. A word of warning: while the website is mostly user-friendly, it's prone to frequent glitches and crashes, so if you're constantly getting error messages, you may need to step away from the computer for a while.

Once your MDE account is up and running, find the "My Plans" link in the pull-down menu and set about entering your ticket, resort, or vacation package confirmation numbers into the appropriate boxes. Disney will request the names and ages of all ticketed members in your party, who will now show up in your "Family & Friends List," allowing you to add them to any future dining or FastPass+ reservations you make going forward. You'll also be able to see any PhotoPass photos taken of these individuals while at Walt Disney World, or after you return home (we'll discuss PhotoPass in Step Nine). As a fun bonus, you can pair each member of your "My Family & Friends" to their favorite Disney avatar.

It's also possible to add other individuals who have their own MDE accounts to your "Family & Friends List." That ability extends to guests you're not lodging with, but who are also traveling to Disney World during your vacation dates, and with whom you'd like to share some PhotoPass photos or vacation plans. If they're not on your list already, "Add a Guest" by entering a friend or family member's reservation confirmation number or by typing in the individual's name. Disney will then use that information to email an invitation to connect your two accounts. Once accepted, you'll automatically see them show up in your "Family and Friends," allowing you to make dining or FastPass+ reservations for everyone in an extended party, whenever that's desirable. This is especially useful for those friends or family members who struggle with technology, or who simply don't want to be responsible for taking the lead on plans.

## ADRs, FastPass+, Memory Maker

If you're within the 180-day window of your Walt Disney World vacation, it's now possible to make or confirm any ADRs at Disney restaurants throughout your stay. If you've already made an ADR by phone with Disney, find the confirmation number and link it under "My Reservations and

Tickets." We'll discuss the ins and outs of making ADRs, especially for the most popular dining locations on Disney property, in Step Eight.

If you're a Disney resort guest, you'll begin making FastPass+ (FP+) reservations for your favorite theme park attractions 60 days prior to your arrival, for the entire duration of your trip. If lodging offsite, your FP+ window opens up 30 days in advance of your stay. As an offsite guest, you must make FP+ reservations one day at a time, progressively, for each day of your trip. We'll discuss the procedure for making FP+ selections, and pin down which ride reservations will save you the most time in lines, in a subsequent chapter.

Finally, if you decide to purchase Memory Maker, Disney's digital photo service that allows you to view, download, and share all Walt Disney World vacation pictures taken by the PhotoPass photographers stationed throughout the parks, in addition to photos taken on select Disney attractions, you may link your Memory Maker confirmation number to your MDE account now, or whenever you purchase the service in the future. In this way, Memory Maker will be activated by the time you hit the parks, allowing you immediate access to every photo Disney takes of your party in the future. We'll dive deeper into Memory Maker's applications in Step Nine.

## Your Itinerary and Wishlist

In the "My Plans" section of My Disney Experience, you can view the reservations and plans you've made for each successive day of your Walt Disney World stay. Once you start building a touring plan that incorporates theme park visits, click the "Add More Plans" link, which will pull up a list of parades, fireworks, shows and character experiences, along with their start times and venues. If the list seems overwhelming at first, filter the options to a preferred park. Have your heart set on seeing Happily Ever After during a Magic Kingdom evening? Locate the show on the list and click "Show in My Plans." That event will now appear in your itinerary, for the day you've selected.

I love this MDE feature. Not only does it lend clarity and structure to your vacation plans, it makes it easy to visually share those plans with friends and family, and invite their feedback. If later on you try to make an ADR or FastPass+ selection that conflicts with another event in your itinerary, Disney will let you know, so you can change it.

Another feature I find especially helpful for first-time visitors to Walt Disney World is the "Wishlist" function in the MDE pull-down menu. When researching the attractions, entertainment, tours, and special events at Disney World within the "Things to Do" menu on Disney's website, you'll see a heart icon next to each item's description. Clicking the heart adds the event to your Wishlist. In this way, you can maintain a list of priorities for any must-do attractions and special events. Take the time to ask your travel companions which attractions and shows they're most interested in exploring, so that by the end of your group's Disney World vacation, everyone will have a collection of favorite experiences to reflect back on.

# MagicBands and Cards

Of all the technological innovations Disney has recently implemented at its Walt Disney World resort, MagicBands have had the greatest impact on guests. So what are these mysterious devices? A MagicBand is a waterproof, adjustable wristband—embedded with an RFID chip—worn by guests of Disney World to:

- quickly board Disney's Magical Express;
- unlock the door of a Disney resort room;
- enter Disney World's theme parks and water parks, and confirm to parking attendants that you're a resort guest;
- secure entrance into FastPass+ attraction lines;
- connect PhotoPass photos to your MDE account;
- charge food and merchandise to your Disney resort account; and
- unlock personalized surprises at select attractions.

MagicBands are mailed at no cost to all Disney resort guests and Annual Passholders. To get yours, go to the "MagicBands and Cards" link in your MDE account, and select the color and

Most Walt Disney World guests will want to experience the classic Pirates of the Caribbean attraction at Magic Kingdom.

inscription (usually a first name) for each member of your travel party, at least 11 days in advance of your trip. Starting in 2019, onsite guests who'd like to upgrade their MagicBands to include novel Disney themes have that option for an average cost of $10/band.

If staying offsite, you have two choices: 1) use the plastic cards sent to you by Disney, or an outside vendor, when purchasing your Walt Disney World tickets, in lieu of MagicBands or 2) purchase MagicBands at https://disneyworld.disney.go.com/store/. A simple MagicBand, without any embellishments, costs $14.99. Alternatively, you can pay a little more for a MagicBand customized with your favorite character or movie tie-in.

Once the MagicBands are in your possession, you'll link them to each person listed in your MDE account. Disney requires you to find the small ID number printed on the inner band to verify your purchase. After you've linked each MagicBand to the ticketed members of your travel party, you're set to go!

Think of your MagicBand as the key to unlocking the door of your MDE account. There is no personal information stored on the band itself. But whenever you arrive at a theme park "touch point," which is a sensor you can touch with your MagicBand to grant you entrance to all theme park, resort room, and FastPass+ attractions, the band's chip will "unlock" your MDE account, and verify that you are where you're supposed to be. If you're staying onsite and have a credit card linked to your room, it will also let you purchase items without using cash or a credit card, and enable Disney's PhotoPass photographers to link any photos taken of your group to your MDE account.

Put on your MagicBand before you leave for the airport, or pack it inside a carry-on bag. If something happens to your checked luggage, you'll be able to head straight to the theme parks, without stopping by Guest Relations for a replacement.

## The MDE App

If you've downloaded the MDE mobile app to your smartphone prior to your trip, you'll have the benefit of carrying all your Walt Disney World vacation plans into the parks, eliminating the need to write down, or memorize, the details of your FastPass+ reservations and ADRs. Hop onto the Disney parks' WiFi network and double check that information in a jiffy by hitting the "My Plans" pull-up menu at the bottom of the screen. I encourage you to familiarize yourself with the app's capabilities before your vacation so you can exploit everything MDE can do for you at the parks.

- **MAPS.** No need to carry around theme park maps anymore when they're right on your phone. Using the menu at the top of the screen, examine the detailed layout of each theme park, or filter the map for its attractions, restaurants, restrooms, shops, PhotoPass photographer locations, special events, and more.

- **PARK HOURS AND TIME GUIDES.** Find out what time the theme park you're visiting closes, when you can catch the next stage show at Cinderella Castle, or where and when to meet favorite characters.

- **WAIT TIMES.** Thinking about riding Frozen Ever After, but don't want to head over there if the line is too long? Check attraction wait times on the app, filtering for "Epcot."

- **CHANGING AND ADDING FP+ SELECTIONS.** Not only can you check and confirm FP+ attraction selections, but you may also change the time—and the attraction itself—on the app, once within Walt Disney World. A further convenience is the ability to add a 4th FP+ selection to your plans after using your first three.

- **CHANGING AND ADDING ADRS.** You can go to "My Plans" to change or cancel an existing dining reservation. (Cancel the night before to avoid a fee.) Clicking on "Reserve Dining" will let you hunt for all available reservations on any given day. You may also review restaurant menus.

- **TRACKING PURCHASES AND DINING CREDITS.** Check the app for records of what you've been charging to your resort account, or jog your memory about the number of dining credits remaining on your Dining Plan.

- **PHOTOS.** Any attraction or PhotoPass photos taken at Walt Disney World will show up almost immediately in your MDE account, under "My Photos."

- **NOTIFICATIONS.** If Disney anticipates an alteration to one of your plans, it will send you a push notification informing you of the change. This usually happens when a ride you have a future FP+ reservation for goes down due to technical problems. If that happens, you'll be allowed to use your FP+ special access anytime after the ride resumes operation.

# Selecting FastPass+ Reservations

Now that your park tickets are linked to your MDE account, you can start planning FastPass+ (FP+) reservations for your upcoming Walt Disney World visit. Before doing so, it's important to understand exactly what FastPass+ is, and how you can put this time-saving tool to work for you.

## How FastPass+ Works

FastPass+ is Disney's free, ride reservation system that allows guests to bypass the standby queues and enter the FP+ line for coveted rides, shows, or character meet-and-greets, where you will typically wait no more than 15 minutes, and often less. Each FP+ reservation window is an hour long, though there is an unspoken "grace period," in which guests may enter the FP+ line five minutes before, and fifteen minutes after, their scheduled time, without being turned away. How does one "check in" to a FP+ reservation? This is where your MagicBand comes in. After holding the band to the FP+ touch point, the Mickey Mouse-shaped sensor will turn green, allowing you entry into the FP+ line, where you may experience the attraction one time. Guests can also use a hard ticket card to enjoy FP+ access.

Each ticketed guest three years of age or older listed in your MDE account may schedule three FP+ reservations per day at Walt Disney World's theme parks. Guests under three may accompany you without a FP+ reservation for attractions in which they meet the height requirement. All three FP+ reservations must be made for the same theme park, although a

4th (and even more) FP+ can be secured for a different theme park after the first three have been used, where a guest has purchased a Park Hopper ticket. With a base ticket, you will make an additional FP+ reservation for the same park you scheduled the first three. These so-called "rolling" FastPasses may show limited availability to guests. FP+ reservations can only be secured during regular park hours, not during Extra Magic Hours or for special events, like parties.

Not every ride or show at Walt Disney World offers FP+ access, and of the ones that do, not all are worth getting. For instance, most FP+ show offerings, in which guests are offered special access or reserved seating, are of scant value. Ideally, you want to select FP+ reservations for attractions that will save you the most time standing in line. The problem comes when every other guest at Disney World wants the same FP+ reservations as you! Later in this chapter, I'll suggest ways to maximize your chances of securing hard-to-get FP+ selections. Guests staying at a Disney World resort (in addition to the Swan and Dolphin and select Disney Springs resorts) may make FP+ reservations 60 days in advance of their first night's stay, starting at 7am EST via the MDE website or app. If an onsite guest has a 5-day ticket, she can make all 15 FP+ reservations at this time, for each guest listed in her account.

This is one of the perks of staying onsite with Disney—and it's a biggie!

Guests staying offsite of Disney property must wait until 30 days before their first theme park visit, and can only make three FP+ reservations per day. In other words, offsite guests have a "rolling" FP+ window. If an offsite guest plans on visiting Disney theme parks on five separate days, and wants to secure FP+ reservations at the earliest possible time for each visit, she will need to make reservations on five separate mornings. This makes it more difficult for offsite guests to nab coveted FP+ reservations for Disney's most popular attractions—difficult, but not impossible, as we'll see later on.

If you're staying onsite, but have guests in your "Family & Friends" who are staying offsite, you may make their FP+ reservations 60 days in advance of your shared trip. This is a big perk for offsite guests traveling with onsite extended family.

Before booking FP+ selections, it's important to research which attractions and character meet-and-greets your family is most keen on experiencing at Walt Disney World. Individual descriptions of the rides and character meets are beyond the scope of this book, so make sure to visit Disney's website and add your favorite attractions to your Wishlist. After building a starter list, you can cross-check your choices with the popular FP+ selections listed below, and find where there's a match.

# Park Planning

One of the main challenges FastPass+ presents to Walt Disney World guests is the necessity of planning out which parks they'll be visiting a month or two in advance of a visit. Not everyone will have the foresight or patience to do this, giving you a potential leg up over those less prepared Disney World vacationers. It's also essential to understand that while a handful of FP+ reservations are difficult to secure, there is wide-ranging availability of most FP+ selections up to, and including, the day of your theme park visit. I have modified our family's FP+ attractions the night before a visit many times, as plans shifted. Other guests will do the same thing, meaning that even hard-to-get FP+ reservations will show a surge in availability during the week approaching your Disney arrival, and especially 24 hours beforehand. The biggest tip I can offer to maximize your chances of getting a tough FP+ reservation is to keep refreshing the website or app. And try not to become overly fixated on securing that one impossible FP+ reservation. If all else fails, you can simply wait in the standby queue.

It's a smart idea to pre-plan your park days in advance of a trip—not only for FP+ reservations, but for dining as well. How should you tackle this planning puzzle? Some put their faith in the prognosticating powers of crowd calendars. On websites like Touring Plans or Undercover Tourist, guests may find park crowd predictions, listed on a 1–10 scale reflecting historical Disney attendance, for the days you'll be visiting the theme parks, in addition to the "recommended" or "not recommended" parks on each day. My opinion? Take these with a grain of salt, as it's getting increasingly difficult to forecast crowd conditions at Walt Disney World, particularly for individual parks on any given day. I find them more useful for giving me a general idea of what crowds will be like the week I'm traveling to Orlando, and not worth rearranging an entire itinerary around.

There are certain, general guidelines you should follow regarding park strategy, however. One of the biggest is to avoid Magic Kingdom on Saturdays, when that park sees peak attendance. If you're staying onsite, find out when Extra Magic Hours (EMH) are, so that you can visit the theme parks while admission is limited to Disney's resort guests. Though you can't book FP+ reservations during EMH hours, that window of time should be used by onsite visitors to ride Disney's most popular attractions. If you're an offsite Walt Disney World guest in possession of a base ticket, you may want to avoid making FP+ selections for parks with EMH hours. Why? Those parks are liable to be busier due to the influx of onsite guests. If, however, you're an offsite guest in possession of a Park Hopper ticket, it's probably fine to book late afternoon or evening FP+ selections for a park with morning EMH hours. The EMH park's increased morning attendance will likely have dissipated by the time of your arrival.

# Making and Modifying FP+ Reservations

The process for making new FP+ selections is easier to understand after logging into the MDE website, hitting the FP+ link, and following Disney's lead. In fact, even if your FP+ window hasn't opened yet, I suggest making a "dummy" FP+ selection for a random date now, which you can cancel later without any harm. That way, you'll know exactly what to do at 7am on the first morning your FP+ window turns active. (Onsite guests with a room/ticket "package" may not have FP+ functionality until their 60 Day FP+ window opens and therefore cannot make a "dummy" reservation.)

For onsite guests who can make all of their trip's FP+ selections at one time, grab the hardest FP+ reservations first, for the final days of your trip. It is exceedingly difficult to nail down an Avatar Flight of Passage FP+, even at 60 days out, so you increase your chances of scoring one if you try for a day that's still—for example—65 days away. Many of your fellow guests won't think to do this, while others may not be enjoying as lengthy a stay. Yes, it's crazy that things are that competitive when it comes to FastPasses—and yet they are! Slinky Dog Dash Roller Coaster, Avatar Flight of Passage, Seven Dwarfs Mine Train, and Frozen Ever After are the hardest FP+ "gets" at Walt Disney World. (Once the Star Wars: Galaxy's Edge attractions acquire FP+ access, expect those to surge to the front of the line.) Trying for them at the end of your trip first will work to your advantage. Do this for all highly coveted FP+ attractions, before filling in other, less contested FP+ selections later.

For onsite and offsite guests, click on the FP+ menu's "Get Started" link to add those members of your party wanting to experience the FP+ attraction you hope to reserve. Guests linked to your MDE account are free to choose different FP+ experiences if they like. After selecting the guests, you'll next see a calendar, from which you can choose the desired date and theme park. A list of FP+ rides, shows, and character meetand-greets will now display, along with a wide range of

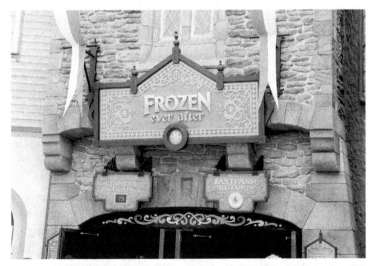

Walt Disney World attractions offering FP+ access
have two separate entrances, one for standby riders
and one for guests with FP+ reservations.

times. If you scroll down to the bottom of the page, you might see experiences marked "currently unavailable." If your attraction is unavailable at this time, make a different FP+ selection you can try to exchange for the desired experience later on.

When making FP+ reservations for Animal Kingdom, Epcot, and Hollywood Studios, you will first be prompted to select a "Tier One" attraction at the top of the page, after which "Other Experiences" are listed. We'll discuss tiering below.

Select the time and attraction you want for your group and then hit "confirm" when prompted. Congratulations! You've just made your first FP+ reservation.

My Disney Experience will then ask if you want to make another FP+ selection, either for the same day or for a different one. And in this fashion, you can continue making all the FP+ reservations allotted to you.

But let's say something happens and you need to alter a FP+ selection later on. If this occurs, bring up your FP+ reservations on either the website or the app. After selecting the attraction you wish to change, Disney will ask if you want to cancel or modify the experience. Cancelling is straightforward enough. But let's say you want to modify the experience instead. First select the guests in your party requiring the modification. Disney will then ask if you'd like to select a different time for the same FP+ experience, or if you want to change the experience entirely. Tweaking the time is easy—Disney will list alternatives. But let's say you're in Epcot and are hoping a Frozen Ever After FP+ has suddenly dropped into the system. You don't want to give up a FP+ you already have, but you'd be eager to make the swap if it suddenly became available. By using the "modify" functionality on your app or the MDE website, you can see what's turned up, and if you do hit the jackpot, make the desired change quickly.

One more thing you can do to increase your odds of securing a hard-to-get FP+ for your entire group is to try and make a FP+ reservation for a single individual only. After confirming the FP+ selection, you can click the "modify" and "add guests" link on the website or app. This sometimes works on the day of a park visit, when Disney's FP+ system is constantly turning over.

*Note*: It's always a good to idea to take a screenshot of your FP+ plans which you can email to yourself if the MDE system misbehaves on the day of a park visit. If you're concerned about your phone battery dying, you can even print it out. In this way, you'll always know where you should be, at what time.

# FastPass+ Tiering

Disney has placed a handful of the most popular attractions in Animal Kingdom, Epcot, and Hollywood Studios into an upper FP+ echelon, Tier One, from which guests may choose a single FP+ reservation, while grouping secondary attractions in Tier Two, from which guests may select two FP+ reservations. In this way, Disney spreads out park crowds by incentivizing guest interest in less obvious attractions. It also means you'll probably have to wait in a standby queue for some popular rides, unless you nab a 4th, "rolling" FP+ selection for a Tier One attraction after using your first three. Fair warning: these are hard to come by. For people hoping to grab one, it's important to position your initial FP+ reservations early in the day, so that some Tier One availability is still available after using your first three. Highly popular attractions, like Avatar Flight of Passage, are nearly impossible to score as a rolling FastPass, while rides like Hollywood Studios' Toy Story Midway Mania or Epcot's Test Track afford a slightly better chance, depending on crowd demand that day.

Check the app for your next "rolling" FastPass selection as soon as you touch the sensor for your last FP+ attraction with your MagicBand. Sometimes, if you're lucky, you can even have your next FP+ window open up as you finish that ride.

# Magic Kingdom

Magic Kingdom has the largest number of attractions and character meet-and-greets offered within Disney's FP+ system. It's also the only park that doesn't order its FP+ offerings within a tiering structure. So in Magic Kingdom you can just make FP+ reservations for those rides and meet-andgreets that will save you the most time waiting in line. With that in mind, here is my ranking of the most desirable FP+ reservations at Magic Kingdom:

- Seven Dwarfs Mine Train
- Peter Pan's Flight
- Space Mountain
- Splash Mountain
- Big Thunder Mountain Railroad

Seven Dwarfs Mine Train, a newer attraction with a wide crossover appeal, is the most difficult FP+ reservation to secure at Magic Kingdom, particularly for offsite guests. The other choices listed should show some availability at 30 days out, though you may not be able to get the exact time you want. Keep trying as the date of your trip draws near. For every other ride or character meet-and-greet at Magic Kingdom, you shouldn't encounter a problem making FP+ reservations, though availability may tighten after most offsite guests confirm their selections.

If you're more interested in meeting characters at Magic Kingdom, these are the most popular meet-and-greets, and consequently the most difficult to nab with a FastPass+:

- Meet Cinderella and a Visiting Princess
- Meet Rapunzel and a Visiting Princess
- Enchanted Tales with Belle
- Meet Mickey at Town Square Theater
- Meet Ariel at Ariel's Grotto

For guests with young children who can't ride any of the "mountains" at Magic Kingdom, character meet-and-greet FP+ reservations offer a great alternative to the more intense rides, as does Enchanted Tales with Belle, a live, interactive storytelling experience particularly appealing to youngsters. Alternatively, if you and your spouse both have your hearts set on riding the more thrilling attractions at Magic Kingdom, but your child/children can't or won't, take advantage of Walt Disney World's rider switch (or "child swap") program, in which one of you rides while another parent waits, before switching up childcare duties to let the other adult experience the attraction without waiting standby. The cast member standing outside the attraction will scan the second adult's MagicBand, granting her special admittance into the FP+ line later. Another great perk of using this system is that up to two children wanting to experience the attraction are usually permitted to ride with both parents, doubling their fun! Just be sure the first group has an initial FP+ reservation for that attraction.

Because of Magic Kingdom's extensive FP+ offerings, and guests' ability to secure multiple "rolling" FP+ selections beyond their first three on most park days, I suggest booking your FP+ reservations for early in the day, starting at 10:00 where park opening is at 9:00. By following this strategy, in which your last FP+ window starts around lunchtime, you will enjoy greater success in nabbing multiple, consecutive rolling FastPasses, for first-rate attractions like Haunted Mansion, Pirates of the Caribbean, and Jungle Cruise. And if the next FP+ window is a little later than you'd like—keep refreshing that app! I promise you, more often than not, something will open up, unless the park is exceptionally crowded.

If you're traveling with a large party, try making a FP+ just for yourself and then "modifying" the FP+ later to incorporate additional guests. Alternatively, group your party's members into several smaller FP+ parties, with overlapping FP+ windows, so everyone can ride together.

# Disney's Animal Kingdom

With the opening of Pandora in 2017, Animal Kingdom switched to a FP+ tiering system, in which its new, prized attractions—Avatar Flight of Passage and Na'vi River Journey—were positioned in Tier One, with all other attractions dropping into Tier Two. As a result, here are the FP+ priorities for most guests enjoying a day at Animal Kingdom:

- Avatar Flight of Passage (Tier One)
- Na'vi River Journey (Tier One)
- Kilimanjaro Safaris
- Expedition Everest (thrill ride; single-rider line available)
- DINOSAUR (scary and not suitable for small children) on cooler days; Kali River Rapids on hot days
- Rivers of Light (reserved seating; nighttime show)

If you can't get a FP+ for Flight of Passage, make a reservation for Na'vi River Journey. Keep checking the app or website to see if you can modify your Na'vi FP+ by exchanging it for Flight of Passage. (Don't cancel, though!) While the Flight of Passage standby queue does add to the overall story, the ride will frequently see wait times of 2–3 hours, and longer. You will breathe a sigh of relief having FP+ for this ride.

A few other attractions offer a single-rider line to guests 7 and up. If you don't mind splitting up your party to ride with people you don't know, you can enjoy lessened wait times. Expedition Everest may be ridden single-rider, so judge accordingly whether you need FP+ for this attraction.

Rivers of Light: We Are One is Animal Kingdom's nighttime show. A FP+ selection here gets you reserved seating access, and can be worthwhile (unless you book a dining package for the show, making FP+ unnecessary). The problem? By selecting a nighttime FP+, you are forfeiting the possibility of securing any rolling FastPasses for the remainder of your day. If that doesn't bother you, Rivers of Light is a fine FP+ investment.

One of the most unique FP+ attractions at Walt Disney World is Kiliminjaro Safaris, which grants Animal Kingdom guests stunning views of its savannah wildlife.

# Epcot

Epcot presents a special challenge to guests making FP+ selections because its top three attractions are all in Tier One. The attractions are Frozen Ever After, Soarin' Around the World, and Test Track. (Priority seating for Epcot's temporary nighttime show, Epcot Forever, will likely have FP+ access, but isn't as essential.) The first two attractions are appealing to guests of most ages, making them hugely popular with families. Test Track is one of only two quasi-thrill rides at Epcot, though its height requirement is less discriminating than those found at other theme parks, making it of especial interest to elementary-aged kids. This confluence of factors makes Epcot FP+ prioritization difficult, but here is the order I'd place them, with caveats:

- Frozen Ever After (Tier One)
- Test Track (Tier One; single-rider line available)
- Soarin' Around the World (Tier One)
- Spaceship Earth (may close for a lengthy refurbishment in early 2020)
- Mission Space or Living with the Land
- Possible character meet-and-greets, coming in September 2019

If you plan on getting to Epcot 30 minutes before park opening, my recommendation is to get a FP+ for Frozen Ever After and head straight to Test Track at rope drop. Why? It's a long trek back to the Norway Pavilion, and with the rest of World Showcase not opening until 11 am., it means having to double back to Future World after finishing. It's best to save yourself some steps and wait to ride Frozen when you're ready to visit that section of the park later in the day.

However, if not arriving ahead of rope drop at Epcot, I'd make Test Track my top FP+ priority, as this attraction has been edging out Frozen for the longest wait times. Either way, I'd save Soarin' Around the World for standby, preferably as close to rope drop as possible, or in the late evening hours.

Another option for those with a Frozen FP+ is riding Test Track single-rider after visiting Soarin' at park opening. This will maximize your touring efficiency of Epcot but you will probably ride Test Track with strangers and won't be able to custom design your vehicle, which is a feature of the ride many guests enjoy.

When arriving at Epcot later in the day, your best bet is to nab a FP+ for Frozen Ever After, use the Test Track single-rider line, and wait standby for Soarin'. Whatever your arrival time, it's not terribly important which pair of Tier Two attractions you plan your FastPasses around. If Spaceship Earth is down for refurbishment, as expected in 2020, I'd stick with Mission Space and Living With the Land. (Mission Space offers two versions of its ride experience: those with motion sensitivity may find the less extreme Green level enjoyable, but claustrophobic guests should avoid the ride entirely).

# Disney's Hollywood Studios

Disney's Hollywood Studios has evolved rapidly with the 2018 unveiling of Toy Story Land, and in 2019 with the opening of Star Wars: Galaxy's Edge, making FP+ selection difficult to predict far into the future. Compounding the confusion, at the end of August 2019, Disney took the unprecedented step of bundling all the park's top FastPass attractions into Tier One, hamstringing guests into choosing just one, with the underlying hope of keeping Star Wars fans spread throughout the park, instead of concentrating themselves in Galaxy's Edge. As such, here are my FP+ priorities for Hollywood Studios in mid-2019, with the caveat that this park's likely to be in a state of flux well into 2020:

- Slinky Dog Dash Roller Coaster (a fun, family roller-coaster appealing to all age groups)
- Rock 'n' Roller Coaster (intense thrill ride; single-rider available)
- Twilight Zone Tower of Terror (intense thrill ride, scary for young children)
- Toy Story Midway Mania (Tier One)
- Alien Swirling Saucers (Tier One)
- Mickey and Minnie's Runaway Railway is slated to open in early 2020, and will likely see high demand if FastPass+ is offered

Slinky Dog Dash Roller Coaster will be most people's preference for a Tier One FP+ selection, since it's a brand-new attraction with a wide demographic appeal. Thrill-ride fans may prefer a go on either Rock 'n' Roller Coaster or Tower of Terror instead. One possible strategy is to utilize the single-rider line for the former, while grabbing a FastPass for Tower of Terror. Toy Story Mania is an interactive hit across all age groups, but doesn't see as long of lines as the first three attractions. Nor does Alien Swirling Saucers, which is a fine ride, if somewhat forgettable.

Star Tours is the only real choice for guests' Tier Two FastPass selection, though Frozen Sing-Along Celebration's FP+ special seating access may be of some benefit to Anna and Elsa fans.

Note: Rolling FastPass+ availability for major attractions will be the silver lining of Disney's new tiering structure at Hollywood Studios. If you're visiting in the morning, stack your FastPasses as early as possible, with the hope of grabbing a valuable 4th Tier One FastPass later on.

The Twilight Zone Tower of Terror at Disney's Hollywood Studios is a terrific FP+ attraction—for guests brave enough to ride it.

# Timing FP+:
# Base Tickets vs Park Hopper

If you have a Magic Your Way base ticket, allowing you to visit one park per day, I would do as much as possible in the morning hours after rope drop and make FP+ reservations for the afternoon hours, when lines are longest. The exception to this rule is Magic Kingdom, where you should secure as many rolling FastPasses as possible by stacking your initial three FP+ selections at 10:00, 11:00, and 12:00 (when park opening is at 9:00).

If you're worried about walking from one side of a park to another in order to make your FP+ window, space your FP+ selections further apart. You may also want to allow extra time for meals and snacks. Remember: for all this "strategy" talk, you're on vacation! I am merely offering guidelines, not suggesting you treat your Walt Disney World vacation like some kind of army drill.

There are two strains of thought regarding FP+ selections with a Park Hopper ticket. Some people like to schedule their FP+ reservations in the morning to increase their chances of securing a Tier One (or highly coveted Magic Kingdom) FP+ at the park to which they're hopping later in the day. I think this is a good strategy for low and moderate crowd level days, when rolling FP+ availability is decent. On very busy days, you're not likely to score a valuable FP+ by noon or early afternoon because they'll all be taken. This would leave you without any FastPasses for the rest of the day, when they're needed most. (The parks are most congested during the afternoon: a good reason to take a resort break!)

Another strategy is to book all FP+ reservations at the second park to which you're hopping later in the day, starting around dinnertime and extending into the evening hours. Facing crowded conditions, you'll enjoy having the security of three FP+s in your pocket. If going this route, it's best to arrive at your first park early in the morning, a half-hour to forty-five minutes prior to rope drop, and get as much park touring in while crowds are light.

# Kiosks

If you don't plan on carrying a smartphone into the parks—or if you run out of battery while doing so—don't worry! You can make or modify FP+ reservations at specially marked kiosks located throughout Disney's theme parks. The kiosks employ touch screens with MagicBand sensors to bring up your MDE account, making it necessary for only one person to be present when altering group plans. One drawback to using a kiosk is that you may only add FP+ selections for the park you're in.

# Technical Problems

If a technical issue crops up with an attraction you have an imminent FP+ for, Disney will send out an email alert notifying you of the problem, and give you 1) the option of returning anytime later in the day to enjoy FP+ entry into the same experience, or 2) offer you the chance to secure a FP+ for a different attraction on the same day. Normally, rides don't stay down for long, so you shouldn't have a problem experiencing the attraction later, though if it's nighttime, you may want to select an alternate experience.

# Booking Advance Dining Reservations (ADRs)

One of the main complaints guests have about taking a Walt Disney World vacation is the need to pin down their trip details so far out in advance. It's easy to imagine a scenario in which someone books a trip less than six months away, unaware that the restaurant she's most looking forward to eating at is unavailable on her trip dates. This is because Disney allows visitors to book ADRs a full 180 days in advance of their table-service meals. If it seems crazy to you to figure out what you want for lunch on a Monday afternoon in Epcot six months from now—rest assured you're not alone.

From Disney's perspective, they see surplus demand for special dining experiences that needs to be culled somehow. By using extended reservation windows, they've decided to reward guests who know the system best, and have done some research in advance. This was definitely not me on our family's first trip to Walt Disney World where, during an afternoon break at Magic Kingdom, I called the reservation line to book a table at Crystal Palace later that evening. I was genuinely surprised to hear there were no tables available. Needless to say, I learned my lesson before our next trip.

Wherever you decide to dine, here are the ADRs you'll need to make as soon as your 180-day reservation window opens:

- Cinderella's Royal Table
- Victoria & Albert's
- Be Our Guest
- California Grill

- Akershus Royal Banquet Hall
- Trattoria al Forno Bon Voyage Breakfast
- 'Ohana
- Chef Mickey's
- Sci-Fi Dine-In Theater Restaurant
- Chef Art Smith's Homecomin' (Disney Springs)

The good news is most Disney restaurants won't require such stringent planning, especially when traveling at off-peak times of the year. I'd also caution against the need to stuff your itinerary full of ADRs, just because you've done your homework. Obviously, if you're on a Disney Dining Plan, you have special incentive to book ADRs. For those guests not on a Dining Plan that uses table-service credits, it's good to make a handful of ADRs for restaurants you're truly excited to eat at, while keeping in mind that ADRs tend to make vacations less flexible, in addition to limiting time at park attractions.

For first-time guests wanting to take in everything a Walt Disney World vacation offers, I'd advise making one ADR for every two to three days of your vacation, and stick with counter-service restaurants otherwise. That said, if you have a family filled with foodies, you might find considerable value in carving out more time for special meals and sampling all the fine cuisine you can squeeze into your stay. Similarly, if you are eager to take advantage of the great photo opportunities afforded with Disney's character meals, by all means schedule some! The more popular character meals on property include Cinderella's Royal Table, Chef Mickey's, Akershus Royal Banquet Hall, 1900 Park Fare, 'Ohana (breakfast), and Garden Grill.

If you're uncertain about committing to an ADR at a Disney table-service restaurant, you can try your luck as a walk-up guest. While most Disney guests, even those with ADRs, will wait around 15 minutes for a table, walk-ups will typically wait 40–75 minutes, and sometimes longer. It really depends on the time of day and crowds. Try mid-afternoon, and other unpopular eating times, if pinning your hopes on walk-up availability. When the parks are busy—or during weeks when free dining is being offered—your chances may be slim for scoring a table. Yet it never hurts to check availability the day-of, or ask your Disney resort concierge to check for you.

Lounges are a fantastic way to enjoy table-service dining without ADRs. Most Deluxe resorts, in addition to other theme park locations, have restaurants with lounges, featuring a wide array of drinks and lighter fare. Some offer select menu items from the restaurant kitchen as well. The famous Cobb Salad at the Hollywood Derby, for example, and a smaller bread service offering at Sanaa, can both be enjoyed without ADRs.

## Where to Eat

My original plan for this chapter was to offer some consensus choices for the best dining options at Walt Disney World, at a range of price points, while tossing in some family favorites as well. I've thought better of this approach for several reasons: 1) there are entire books devoted to dining at Walt Disney World; 2) when it comes to food, taste is incredibly subjective;

Epcot's World Showcase offers a number of fine dining options, including Les Chefs de France.

3) there is a mind-boggling range of dining experiences found at Disney, from character meals and dessert parties, to snack items and resort room service; and 4) as many times as I've visited Walt Disney World, the number of restaurants I haven't eaten at far exceeds the ones I've been able to enjoy.

Instead of stuffing this chapter full of information found elsewhere, I suggest you check out out the current menus on Disney's website by clicking the "All Dining" link and filtering the options to your tastes. For example, if you want to see where you can meet Disney characters, select "Character Dining" in the "Dining Experience" pull-down menu. The website will tell you what kind of meal (counter-service or table-service) you can enjoy at each establishment, the restaurant's location, and the price you'll pay for a typical entree.

# Using My Disney Experience to Make ADRs

If you're keen to book ADRs for Disney's most popular dining experiences, be prepared to have logged into your MDE account by 6am EST on the morning your 180-day ADR window opens, with credit card in hand. If you've already booked a room at a Disney resort, you should be able to schedule 180+10 days' worth of ADRs for your upcoming Walt Disney World stay at this time. As we saw with FP+ reservations, onsite guests will enjoy the greatest success in booking their hardest-to-get reservation first, for a time near the end of their stay. This is because offsite guests have a "rolling" ADR window, and must make reservations day by day, for the length of their stay. So if a Disney resort guest and an offsite guest were to take identical trips over the same week, and they both wanted to eat at Cinderella's Royal Table on the sixth day of their vacations, the onsite guest is more likely to secure the reservation since she can book it 186 days before her meal, instead of 180. Again, Disney wants to make it worth your while to stay onsite, and this is an incentive toward doing so. (If you run into a snag online, call the 407-WDW-DINE reservation line, starting at 7am EST, instead.)

To make your first ADR, find "Things to Do" on the MDE website, and under Dining, select "Make Reservations." Type the name of the restaurant into the search box. After it loads, plug in your date, meal time, and party size (up to 14 people) for the desired dining experience. Disney allows you to select times in half-hour increments, or around broader meal times, like "Dinner." Try both if you don't have luck using the first method. After entering your preferences, Disney will tell you if there are any tables available for your party at that time. If there are, select the desired time. If not, you can input an alternate time or date, or try again later.

After finding a time slot you're happy with, select the names of the guests dining with you. If listing yourself as the "lead guest," know that only you'll be able to cancel the reservation later on. Disney will ask if you have any special dietary requests to make. Be sure to mark down the food allergies and sensitivities of the people you're traveling with. Later, when being seated, you can remind the restaurant's hostess of any special requests. Walt Disney World is exceptionally accommodating of their guests' allergies and food sensitivities, so there should never be a problem fulfilling a request. For kosher or halal meals, call (407) WDW-DINE at least 24 hours before a reservation. It's also best to call the Disney dining line at least 48 hours in advance, if planning a special celebration for which you're ordering a custom cake.

Take a screenshot of all your ADRs to email to yourself, or print. Disney will send you an emailed reminder 24 hours in advance of your dining reservation. It's important to have your reservation number handy when traveling by car to a Disney resort restaurant, since the parking guards may ask for it. Once admitted, you'll have three hours to enjoy a meal.

If you're looser about the ADRs you wish to book, don't bother searching for a specific restaurant on the Disney website. Instead, after selecting "Make Reservations" in the "Dining" menu, plug in a date and meal time, filtering the options according to type of meal, price range, cuisine variety, and/or theme park location. A list of available restaurants will pop up, and you can scan the choices for the most appealing options. This is especially helpful the closer you get to your theme park arrival date, when most restaurant tables are booked, and you're forced to get creative.

It's amazing how often Walt Disney World guests will find a new, favorite restaurant, after trying to secure an ADR at a beloved old favorite and coming away empty-handed. There are so many unique and wonderful restaurants at Walt Disney World; try not to pin all your hopes on just a handful of popular choices. You might very well find something you like even better.

# Restaurants Requiring Prepayment in Full

Disney requires a credit card to book and hold dining reservations. While most restaurants won't charge your card unless you fail to show up—thus incurring the dreaded $10/person cancellation charge—there are a handful of dining experiences requiring full payment in advance: Cinderella's Royal Table, Hoop-Dee-Do Musical Revue Dinner Show, Polynesian Spirit of Aloha Dinner Show, Disney Girl's Perfectly Princess Tea Party, and the Magic Kingdom Fireworks Dessert Party.

Refunds are offered when cancelling at least 24–48 hours in advance of your meal (individual restaurants vary, so check your terms). If using Disney Dining Plan credits to pay for an experience, you may still be asked for a credit card number. Make sure your Magic Your Way package confirmation number has been linked to your MDE account so that Disney "knows" you'll be using Dining Plan credits and won't charge the price of the meal in advance. If, by some fluke, it looks like your credit card will be charged, abort your online booking attempt and take the time to call 407-WDW-DINE instead to confirm the reservation.

# Group Dining

With peak demand for ADRs, it can be especially difficult for Disney guests traveling with a large party to get their foot in the door. If you find yourself in this situation, and haven't been able to secure a reservation online, my suggestion is to call the dining line at 407-WDW-DINE and request assistance with "Group Dining." You'll then be transferred to a Disney cast member happy to sweat the details for you. Often, this might mean breaking your large party into smaller groups, each with its own reservation, and asking the restaurant's hostess to seat you at adjacent tables. It might also behoove you to book your meal at an off-peak time, or to try a restaurant more amenable to large gatherings.

It's important to ask each member of your dining party about food allergies or sensitivities before taking the lead on booking ADRs. You should also be relatively certain everyone will show up to the restaurant on time. Finally, know that it's customary for Disney to add an 18% gratuity to the bill for groups larger than 6, even when on the Dining Plan.

## Using the MDE App

When setting up your initial ADRs, I recommend using the MDE website, since you can filter the dining experiences to your preferences, and search for specific restaurants within Disney's database. However, once you're actually at Walt Disney World, it's easy to switch over to the MDE app to see which restaurants are showing availability. Just click on "Reserve Dining," enter in your party size, the date and time you wish to dine, and Disney will bring up a list of restaurants with open tables. This is a great way of keeping tabs on any last-minute ADRs that open up.

## Changes and Cancellations

If you need to reschedule your ADR for a different day or time—or change the size of your dining party—you may do so via the MDE website or the app. Simply find your reservation and select "change" (website) or "modify" (app). Disney will let you know if there is availability matching your new preferences.

If you wish to cancel an ADR, make sure you do so by midnight on the night before your reservation (cancellation windows vary, so check your ADR terms closely), or Disney will charge you a $10/person fee for being a no-show. You may cancel the ADR online through your MDE website or app, or by calling 407-WDW-CNCL. I'd recommend the latter route if you made your initial dining reservation via phone or if you're cutting it close to the cancellation window.

Guests dining at Magic Kingdom's Be Our Guest restaurant may enjoy the beautiful atmosphere as much as the food.

If it's the day of your ADR, and you don't think you'll be able to make it to the restaurant on time, call 407-WDW-DINE to see if a cast member can help you find an earlier or later dining time, allowing you to keep your reservation without incurring a penalty. It's aways easier to speak with a real person if there are extenuating circumstances needing to be explained.

# Last-Minute Reservations

Not able to nail down that ADR you really wanted? Keep trying, as Disney's reservation system is constantly in flux. If you're an onsite guest trying to make an ADR more than 180 days before a desired dining experience, try again at the 180-day mark. Sometimes Disney will open up more tables for offsite guests at this time.

If you're already at Walt Disney World, check availability the night before you'd like to eat at a specific restaurant. There is often a flurry of last-minute cancellations the night before the meal you're hoping to reserve, and you stand a decent chance of nabbing a table if you keep refreshing the app. If you're visiting a park, and see a restaurant you're interested in, pull out your phone and check MDE. There might just be a table with your name on it inside.

There are several non-Disney-owned restaurants in Disney Springs, and at the Swan and Dolphin resorts, which aren't a part of Disney's reservation system. If you'd like to eat at one of these establishments, google their phone numbers and place a direct call to the restaurant to reserve your table in advance.

Still coming up empty-handed? Here are your best bets for dining without an ADR at Walt Disney World:

- Yak & Yeti or Rainforest Café at Animal Kingdom
- San Angel Inn, Nine Dragons, Biergarten, Restaurant Marrakesh, or Spice Road Table at Epcot
- Jungle Skipper Canteen at Magic Kingdom
- Mama Melrose at Hollywood Studios
- Olivia's (Old Key West), Kona Café (Polynesian Resort), Grand Floridian Café (Grand Floridian), The Wave (Contemporary Resort), Trail's End (Fort Wilderness), Maya Grill (Coronado Springs)

# Special Dining Events

There are a few unique dining experiences at Walt Disney World deserving of special mention, as they offer considerable value beyond the meal itself:

**PRE-PARK-OPENING BREAKFASTS.** These meals are offered at select restaurants in every theme park. The only hitch? Getting up early enough to meet your reservation! Make sure you have your dining confirmation number to show the cast members at the park entrance gates, who will let your party through about 75 minutes before official park opening. This is a great way to see (and photograph) the parks when they're nearly empty, and a fun, special way to start a Disney day. For me, the best of these meals is the one served at Be Our Guest in Magic

Kingdom. Not only can you enter Magic Kingdom earlier than other park guests, affording you fantastic photo opportunities in front of Cinderella Castle, you will also enjoy a delicious breakfast inside the Beast's Fantasyland castle— one of the most exquisite settings in all of Walt Disney World—for a single quick-service credit on the Dining Plan. (You may order ahead of time to streamline the process.) But that's not all. If you time things right, and finish your breakfast by 8:45am, you can slip into the nearby Seven Dwarfs Mine Train line before the park officially opens. The cast members will let you ride the attraction before other guests start streaming in, which is a big bonus, considering how quickly the line builds for this ride. Afterward, you can hop over to Peter Pan's Flight, or another attraction, giving you an amazing jumpstart to your Magic Kingdom touring day.

**DINING PACKAGES FOR SHOWS.** If you're a firm believer that time is money on a Walt Disney World vacation, you might think about reserving a dining package for one of Disney's nighttime shows, which will not only get you reserved seating access for the show—saving you precious time in line—but will also secure you a reservation for lunch or dinner at one of Disney's many fine table-service restaurants in Animal Kingdom, Hollywood Studios, or, depending on the time of year, Epcot. Dining packages are also available for the afternoon parade at Magic Kingdom and for Festival of the Lion King at Animal Kingdom. Reserving a dining package can be particularly cost-effective for guests using table-service credits on the Disney Dining Plan. They also alleviate the need to secure a FP+ reservation for the same show.

**DESSERT PARTIES.** Held nightly at all four theme parks, these special dessert parties—offering VIP viewing for the nighttime shows—have become hugely popular with Disney World guests over the years. I recommend them for people looking to mark a special occasion, or for those guests with mobility issues who don't want to worry about staking out a viewing spot far ahead of a show's start time (though not all dessert parties offer seating). Whatever your reason for booking a dessert experience, you're sure to indulge in a wide array of sweet and savory food items themed to that park's nighttime show, as well as enjoying the many specialty drinks on hand (hot and cold beverages, alcohol included). However, these are pricey events to book for an entire family. If I were to recommend one, I'd give the nod to Star Wars: A Galactic Spectacular Dessert Party at Hollywood Studios. Held in the Star Wars Launch Bay, it's the best-themed event of the bunch. Stormtroopers will even escort you to your fireworks viewing spot—and it's hard to beat that!

**FIREWORKS WHILE DINING.** Don't want to break the bank on an elaborate dessert party? Dining at a restaurant offering a partial fireworks view might be the answer you're looking for. Epcot's nightly show lends itself especially well to this strategy, since the fireworks are launched from the World Showcase lagoon, in sight of many popular restaurants like Rose & Crown, La Hacienda de San Angel, Tokyo Dining, Monsieur Paul, and Spice Road Table. It's best to make your dining reservation about 90 minutes before showtime. And be mindful of the fact that while you may request a table with a fireworks view, it won't always be possible for the hostess to accommodate you. Feel free to let her know you're willing to wait for optimal seating. If you can't snag an ADR for a table-service restaurant at Epcot, try the counter-service option of Cantina de San Angel in Mexico. For the Happily Ever After fireworks show at Magic Kingdom, your best bet is to dine at a location outside of the park itself. The number-one place to go? California Grill at Disney's Contemporary Resort. Narcoosee's at the Grand Floridian and 'Ohana at the Polynesian also offer partial fireworks views—if you can nab a window table. Be aware that the Cinderella Castle projections are a big part of Happily Ever After, and can't be seen outside of the park.

# Mobile Ordering

One of my favorite new features of the MDE app is the ability to order food in the parks, eliminating the need to stand in line. While it's long been possible to order your Be Our Guest breakfast or lunch up to 30 days ahead of a Magic Kingdom visit, Disney has expanded its mobile ordering service to include twenty-seven counter-service restaurants in the parks.

How do you order a meal through MDE? Simple. Let's say you're in Animal Kingdom, waiting in line for the Na'vi River Journey attraction. You have a hankering to try the protein bowls you've heard so much about at Satu'li Canteen nearby. Problem is, there was a huge line when you happened by the restaurant entrance earlier. No problem! Just pull out your smartphone, bring up the MDE app, and tap "Order Food." Find Satu'li Canteen in the Animal Kingdom section to bring up its menu. Select the items your party wants (not exceeding $150), and when you're finished, tap "Purchase." Disney will then charge the credit card linked to your MDE account. Immediately thereafter, you'll receive an order confirmation—and, voilà! You've wisely used your time in one line to prevent yourself from having to stand in another. The restaurant won't start preparing your food until you tap the "I'm Here, Prepare My Order" link on the app. There's no need to be physically inside the restaurant to do this—feel free to peruse a nearby gift shop or use the restroom while your food is being made. After a few minutes, you'll receive a push notification—and text message—that your order is ready, at which point you can walk to the counter via the "Mobile Order Pick Up" sign and pick up your food.

This is a quick and easy tool any Walt Disney World guest can take advantage of, especially when counter-service restaurant lines are at their longest.

# Making a Date with Memory Maker

In our house, there's one family photo I look at more than any other. It sits atop our living room bookshelf and features the four of us, bundled in sweatshirts—but smiling broadly—on a chilly Florida morning on Main Street, U.S.A. In the background are the soaring spires of Cinderella Castle. The photo was taken by a Disney PhotoPass photographer and whenever I see it, I'm reminded of our family's January trip from five years ago. More importantly, though, it feels like a placeholder for all our wonderful Walt Disney World memories, and a visual promise of more trips to come.

The funny part about that photo, though, is that I did not purchase Memory Maker—Disney's digital download package—to get it. Instead, we bought it as a standalone photo from Disney's PhotoPass service. Which leads to the question I'm sure you're asking right about now: just what is the difference between PhotoPass and Memory Maker?

## PhotoPass

Disney's PhotoPass service is simply that—a complimentary photography service any Walt Disney World guest can use to have their vacations documented at picturesque spots throughout the four theme parks and two water parks, and at select resorts, character meals, and meet-and-greets.

How does it work? Disney employs dozens of PhotoPass photographers—easy to spot with their tan vests and DSLR cameras—to take guests' photos throughout their Walt Disney

World stays. Generally, you can find photographers' locations by touching the "PhotoPass" link at the top of the MDE app. If you'd like your picture taken by a Disney PhotoPass photographer, all you have to do is approach one and ask. (At popular locations, like Cinderella Castle, you may have to wait a bit.) If you have a MagicBand, the photographer will scan it with an RFID scanner to link the photo automatically to your My Disney Experience (MDE) account, where it should show up soon after. Photos taken of any "Family & Friends" members linked to your account will also appear there, as long as those members have a MagicBand, hard ticket, or an Annual Pass card capable of being scanned. If the group member does not have one of these things, the photographer will hand her a PhotoPass card with an ID number on it that can later be entered into an MDE account, bringing up all photos associated with that number online.

Disney photographers can also take Magic Shots. These are photos of your family with Disney characters digitally inserted into the mix. If you'd like a Magic Shot, simply ask for one. Disney photographers are great at eliciting a specific reaction, and it's a lot of fun to see the end results. Kids especially get a big kick out of seeing Olaf or Tinker Bell show up alongside them—and it's a novel way of bringing home some Disney magic from your trip.

You are welcome to use PhotoPass as much as you like, without paying a dime. The photos Disney takes will remain in your account, with watermarks on them, until 45 days after their time stamp. The price of downloading a single photo is $16.95, which you can then print yourself or send off for printing. Select Disney attractions offer on-ride photos, which are a lot of fun, since they're often taken at a big, high-impact moment, like the drop in Splash Mountain. If you have a MagicBand, you don't have to do a thing for these photos to appear in your MDE account. If you don't have a MagicBand, you'll want to scan your ticket or PhotoPass card beneath the screens at the end of the ride to upload a ride photo to your account. Just look for the screen with your picture on it.

At press time, two attractions—Seven Dwarfs Mine Train and Twilight Zone Tower of Terror—offer on-ride videos, with magical introductions seamlessly melding your ride experience into the larger Disney story. You must have a MagicBand to access these videos via MDE. Undoubtedly, Disney will bring more of these crowd-pleasing videos to life on other attractions in years to come.

Disney PhotoPass photographers are friendly, accommodating professionals, and the quality of their high-resolution shots is superb. Prints as large as 16x20 will offer sharp clarity and good color balance. Most importantly, PhotoPass photographers are great at anticipating the magic moments at hand during character meet-and-greets. They'll get down on your child's level to take a range of shots, ensuring parents get the one. And when you have a small child preparing to meet Mickey Mouse for the first time, that's exactly the kind of ally you want. No need to fumble with your phone's camera and miss the magic as it's unfolding. Now you can experience the moment while being secure in the knowledge it's been recorded for posterity, too.

All PhotoPass photos are organized in your MDE account by their theme park setting, or other Walt Disney World location. I suggest downloading most of the large files onto a computer, although you're free to download a few onto your phone to share via social media or email. Disney offers some photo-editing capabilities that let you zoom in or change a photo's orientation. Before doing any editing, make sure to "create a copy" of the image first, so you'll have the unedited version in your account. You can also add various fun, Disney-themed borders and stickers to any photo you wish to embellish. If you decide to purchase and download a photo for $16.95, be sure to do it within that 45-day window after the photo was taken.

You may order prints from Disney, or purchase personalized items like phone cases, mugs, or magnets from the Disney PhotoPass website. For a cheaper alternative, simply download the photo and use Shutterfly or another retailer to order comparable products. Disney will provide you a copyright release of all PhotoPass images for any personal, non-commercial use. Make a habit of checking the photos in your MDE account throughout your trip to ensure they're showing up. If a photo is missing—or the animation hasn't been incorporated into a Magic Shot—call Disney's PhotoPass support line at 407560-4300 to remedy the problem.

# Memory Maker

Memory Maker is Disney's unlimited digital photo package, enabling Walt Disney World guests to download as many of their vacation PhotoPass images as they want. The service is $169 when purchased in advance, $199 if you wait until the trip, or shortly after. You can buy Memory Maker through Disney's website, by phone, or at select locations at Disney World or in Disney Springs; if you go the latter route, you'll have to link Memory Maker to your MDE account before the photos will appear. The service may be included as part of select Disney packages as well. When buying your package in advance, make sure you purchase it at least three days before your trip, or you may miss out on some initial shots.

Is Memory Maker worth the investment? Generally, yes. Most people who purchase Memory Maker are glad they did so. If you take full advantage of the PhotoPass system, you can have hundreds of vacation photos by the time you come home. Now, do you need hundreds of vacation photos? Probably not, but few folks are going to be sorry to have them, and chances are excellent you'll have many memorable, poignant, and/or thrilling shots chronicling a specific moment in time, never to be repeated, with the people you love at a very special place.

Our family's 2018 spring break visit to Magic Kingdom will live on thanks to Memory Maker.

Memory Maker includes all on-ride photos and videos. The nice thing about the package is that only one member of a "Friends & Family" cohort needs to buy the service for each guest to see everyone else's photos, whether they're in that shot or not. While only the person purchasing Memory Maker can download and edit photos, it's pretty simple to send those files off to others, making Memory Maker's price point much more reasonable when several parties can benefit from a single transaction. Don't want other people in your "Family & Friends" seeing your photos? Disney lets you "uncheck" the photo sharing box with guests in MDE accounts that are linked to yours if you'd rather keep those memories private.

Memory Maker will be especially valuable for guests who:

- are first-time visitors to Walt Disney World;
- are enjoying an extended vacation;
- plan on meeting a lot of Disney characters, either at meet-and-greets or at character meals (check before-hand to see if PhotoPass photographers will be present);
- take part in special experiences like Bibbidi Bobbidi Boutique, Jedi Training Academy, Pirate's League, etc.;
- are celebrating the holidays or another special occasion; or
- want a more formal, structured photo shoot at the Disney PhotoPass Service Studio at Disney Springs.

Your Memory Maker credit is activated whenever you begin downloading pictures. After initiating, you have 30 days to complete all photo downloads, so make sure you only activate Memory Maker when you're ready to tackle your digital scrap-booking head-on.

Still on the fence? Maybe a little math will help:

- If you can see yourself wanting at least 10 theme park, ride, or character photos while vacationing at Walt Disney World, pre-purchasing Memory Maker through your MDE account is the way to go.
- If you'd rather wait and see how your vacation photos will turn out, Memory Maker will still be a worthy investment if you find at least 12 photos to download during or after your trip.

Not everyone will want to spend that kind of money on vacation photos, especially if you already have a good, willing photographer in your travel group. Who else might think twice before purchasing Memory Maker?

- Guests taking short vacations
- Shy folks who aren't keen on posing for strangers
- Guests not interested in Disney's character interaction
- Vacationers on a limited budget

# Annual Passholders

A major enticement toward purchasing a Disney World Annual Pass is that a Memory Maker equivalent is included in the price of your pass—but with the added benefit of keeping photos in your MDE account for a year before downloading. This benefit often adds up to more than its $169 sticker cost, since Annual Passholders are liable to take more than one Disney World vacation during that time period. Even for families who plan on a one-time visit, upgrading to an Annual Pass can some- times be worthwhile when you count up all the discounts and perks Disney includes with their Annual Pass program, espe- cially since only a single member of a travel party need become an Annual Passholder for everyone to reap the benefits.

Every PhotoPass photo—whether taken of your immedi- ate family or of the "Family & Friends" linked to your MDE account—can be downloaded by the Annual Passholder across his 365-day membership span. As was the case with Memory Maker, the Annual Passholder is responsible for downloading and sharing the photos with other members of his group.

If you decide to upgrade your Magic Your Way ticket to an Annual Pass while visiting Walt Disney World, and you've already purchased Memory Maker in advance, Disney may credit the cost of your Memory Maker purchase into the upgrade, meaning you won't have to pay for the same service twice

# Developing a Touring Plan

The amount of planning one does in advance of a Walt Disney World trip tends to fall on opposite ends of a spectrum: the people who do too much, needlessly stressing themselves out over the most minute details of their itineraries, and guests who don't enjoy their trips as much as they might, because they don't have the foggiest notion about dining and FP+ reservations, much less what time they should be showing up for Extra Magic Hours or rope drop.

Fortunately, there's plenty of room between these two extremes, and it's my intention to help you find that Goldilocks, " just right" level of preparedness. Walt Disney World vacations have become more complicated over the last decade, but that doesn't mean you can't make flexibility and spontaneity a priority in your personal plans as well. If your expectations are too rigid by the time you get to Orlando, any deviation from that plan is liable to feel more like a disappointment than an opportunity. Keep that in mind as you peruse the advice in this chapter—and be sure to write down your itinerary in pencil, not ink.

## Park Day Guidelines

Because of the need to schedule FP+ reservations and ADRs in advance, I'm a big believer in having a game plan for which parks you'll be visiting most days, in addition to scheduling at least one "down" day for longer trips. These plans can be altered later, but there's a degree of security in having a pocket full of FP+ reservations, and some dining arrangements, during even the busiest seasons at Walt Disney World.

Here are some other factors to consider when creating an itinerary:

- Look at the number of days you're spending at the four main theme parks. Does it reflect your groups' interests in the attractions and entertainment offered there? If you started a My Disney Experience "Wishlist" back in Step Six, consult it now to see which park experiences you're most eagerly anticipating. For first-time guests, especially those with young children, spending the greatest number of days at Magic Kingdom is a no-brainer. The park has by far the most attractions and feels the most iconically "Disney" to guests. On the other hand, Epcot's diversity of attractions and culinary riches make it especially enticing to older guests. Animal Kingdom is a big draw for animal lovers, of course, but also showcases a wealth of inspiration from African and Asian cultures, and has a marvelous new offering in Pandora. Finally, Disney's Hollywood Studios is a park with the wind at its back, thanks to guests' surging interest in Star Wars: Galaxy's Edge and Toy Story Land.

- Consult park maps before you visit Walt Disney World to familiarize yourself with their layouts. Check the height restrictions for rides if you have small children. Make a note of which attractions you'll be using Disney's rider-switch service that allows you (and any child meeting the height requirement) to ride, while another adult waits with the non-riding child, before switching things up so the other adult can ride, too. Consider any single-rider lines you plan on using: Expedition Everest in Animal Kingdom, Test Track in Epcot, and Rock 'n' Roller Coaster in Hollywood Studios all offer this expedited waiting process for solo guests.

- Don't plan too much for your arrival day, especially when it comes to scheduling ADRs you might miss due to a travel setback. This could be a great time to explore your resort, go swimming, visit a water park, or head to Disney Springs. Similarly, don't cut things too close on your departure day if your plans include a theme park visit. Remember, if you're staying onsite and using Disney's Magical Express bus service for airport transportation, you'll need to be back at your resort, ready for pickup, three hours before a flight.

- If your lengthier stay includes a weekend, schedule a day away from the parks on Saturday, when the four theme parks—and especially Magic Kingdom—are busiest.

- Look at the Extra Magic Hours (EMH) schedule in advance, even as an offsite guest. Parks tend to be more crowded on days offering this extra touring time to Disney's resort guests. If you want to experience morning EMH, it's best to have a Park Hopper ticket that allows you to spend some initial time at the EMH park, before hopping elsewhere later. A clever strategy to follow for guests planning lengthier vacations—in which EMH is not as much a priority—is to visit whichever park had EMH hours the day before. It's unlikely onsite guests will bounce back to the same park two days in a row.

- Special events—like parties, celebrations, and festivals—may impact park visits. It's best to avoid the local-friendly Epcot festivals on Saturdays and Sundays. If traveling to Magic Kingdom on the day of a ticketed party you won't be attending, understand that you will have to leave the park by 6pm. If your group plans on participating in a party, holiday celebration, tour, festival, or special dining experience, schedule those now so you know which day you'll be visiting that park. As far as entertainment goes, things are simpler: the parks' parades and nightly shows usually have consistent, daily showtimes across most guests' vacation stays.

- Park hours should be consulted when forming an initial itinerary (though they're subject to change). If you're eager to close down a park some night, see which parks offer extended hours, and when. Alternatively, if you've scheduled a pre-park-opening breakfast in order to take advantage of the benefits discussed in Step Eight, be sure that park isn't opening an hour earlier than usual, for EMH or some other reason.

- Water parks are a fun diversion during the afternoon, or on any "down" day you spend away from the four major parks. Of course, spending several hours baking in the Florida sun might tire you out more than you'd think! When visiting Blizzard Beach, consider a turn at the neighboring Winter Summerland's miniature golf course.

- Which items will you most need inside the parks? Try not to weigh yourself down with superfluous extras, especially during the hottest months. But start making a packing list now, so you have time to order essentials. Are you planning on bringing food into the parks? Consider the lockers offered to Walt Disney World guests, and whether the added expense is necessary.

- It's sometimes nice to hold back a special experience until the last full day of your Disney vacation. A lot of people— myself included—start getting a little sad as a trip comes to an end, so having a fun, unique experience to look forward to on that last day helps keep your spirits up.

# Park Touring Strategy

Are you an early bird or a night owl? The answer to this question may impact your Walt Disney World visit more than you think. Because park crowds don't start building until late in the morning, early risers have a built-in advantage toward experiencing the greatest number of Disney attractions in the least amount of time. While crowds will eventually dissipate throughout the evening hours, there's just no doubt that wait times for rides are shortest right at park opening.

In fact, even though our teenage daughter would love to sleep in on our vacations, she's willing to do the very un-teen-age thing of getting up at 7:00am because she knows how much more we get done during those first two hours of park time, when temperatures are also coolest. Participating in rope drop—in which you arrive at a theme park 15–60 minutes prior to park opening—is a great way of maximizing your ride or character interaction time at Disney World. Yes, you'll have to invest some extra time waiting at the park gates—or just inside them—at the beginning of your day. This small investment pays off big dividends later on, allowing you to slow down and enjoy some second-tier attractions when others are stuck waiting in the longest lines of the day.

A quick in-room breakfast is often the right call for early starters—both for your budget and schedule. Buses typically start running from Disney's resorts just before 7:00am for a 9:00 open, in order to accommodate guests with ADRs, so getting there with time to spare shouldn't be difficult. The first buses to arrive will be bound for Magic Kingdom, with the others following close behind.

All that being said, you are on vacation. If it's stressful to imagine waking yourself—and everyone else—up at the crack of dawn each day, just so you can get in more rides at rope drop, don't do it. Touring Disney World with a large group already presents some unique challenges. Asking everyone to be ready at the same early time in the morning could lead to resentments and, ultimately, vacation burn-out. Arriving later in the day might even make sense for guests with a Magic Your Way base ticket, who don't want to take a mid-afternoon break and wish to stay through park closing.

## Park Entry

Before the entrance of every Walt Disney World theme park is a row of tables staffed by Disney security guards who check guests' bags for prohibited items. Not everyone needs to go through "bag check," but if you have any sort of bag—even a fanny pack—you'll be required to, and should allot a few extra minutes in your touring plan. Members of your party without bags can use the bagless entrance, though guests of either circumstance will still have to pass through a metal detector.

Magic Kingdom's security protocol is slightly different. If arriving at the park via the monorail, guests will go through bag check and security prior to boarding, either at the Transportation & Ticket Center or at a monorail resort. Guests arriving by bus will still be screened at the park entrance.

As you approach the turnstile to enter a park, you'll be required to scan your MagicBand or hard ticket at the RFID reader. Next, you'll be prodded to place your index finger on a touch pad to record the geometric pattern unique to your fingerprint, in order to link you to your ticket. (Don't worry—Disney won't have your exact fingerprint on record.) If the scan computes your finger pattern correctly, the Mickey head on the turnstile will turn green. If it turns blue, a Disney cast member will ask you to try again. Sometimes, the system is temperamental and requires multiple attempts to get right.

# Magic Kingdom Rope Drop Procedures and Priorities

With over thirty attractions, and a wide variety of character meet-and-greets, Magic Kingdom is a park best enjoyed over two or more days of a Walt Disney World vacation. In fact, it's not unusual for first-time visitors to spend half of their park time at this most popular Orlando destination.

Even on a 9:00 o'clock park opening day, ticketed guests will be let onto Main Street just before 8:00, and stopped near the hub, a grassy area in front of Cinderella Castle from which the park's five main lands diverge. Guests with breakfast ADRs will have a few extra minutes inside the park, being typically admitted around 7:45. Even for guests without ADRs, that first morning hour at Magic Kingdom is worth savoring. Disney's PhotoPass photographers are available to ensure some stellar shots of your group in front of the castle. Shops and restaurants on Main Street are also open, so if you didn't have time to grab breakfast or coffee at your hotel, now's your chance to pick up something while you wait for the park's official opening show to begin at 8:55am. The show is a brief, charming appearance by Mickey, Minnie, and Co., welcoming you into the park with the assistance of some magic from the Fairy Godmother's wand.

Most Magic Kingdom rope droppers will head first to Seven Dwarfs Mine Train, Peter Pan's Flight, or, to a lesser degree, one of the "mountains" (Space, Big Thunder, and Splash). When facing the castle, you'll want to take the path to the right (not through the castle) to get to Seven Dwarfs Mine Train quickest.

If you're headed to Peter Pan's flight, cut through the castle itself. The crowds may seem daunting as you're waiting for the welcome show to start, but the throng breaks up quickly as everyone scatters in various directions at rope drop. If you plan on riding Seven Dwarfs Mine Train first, you must be inside the park, stationed to the right of the castle, by around 8:15 a.m., or the benefits of a rope-drop strategy will be nulled. The line for that attraction builds fast. If you're a little slower than anticipated with your arrival, you should abandon the notion of riding Mine Train, because the first hour of your Magic Kingdom day is too precious to spend standing in line. For that reason—and because of some stress involved in rope-dropping Seven Dwarfs Mine Train—I recommend getting a FP+ reservation instead. Doing so may mean a later wake-up time for your party as well. In order to rope drop Seven Dwarfs Mine Train effectively, you should start waiting for a Disney resort bus by 7:15 to ensure you get inside the park within the hour. (If you just missed a bus, for instance, you may have to wait 20 minutes for the next.) For offsite guests, there is the additional hassle of having to park, walk (or take a tram) to the Transportation & Ticket Center, where you will pass through security before waiting for the monorail. For this reason, Magic Kingdom has the most onerous entrance procedure for offsite visitors. You should allot extra time as a result.

Guests who make it to Magic Kingdom by 7:20 for an 8:00 opening will find their morning touring efficiency substantially increased, as most vacationers won't match your enthusiasm for early rising.

A large percentage of Disney World guests spend their first hour in Fantasyland, because it has a high concentration of rides and character meet-and-greets, making touring there compact and easy. Alternatively, if you're not as interested in rides aimed squarely at the younger set, and would rather head to Frontierland to get in multiple rides on Big Thunder Mountain Railroad and Splash Mountain, before crossing over to Adventureland, that's an excellent use of a first hour, too. The final possibility is to hit Space Mountain in Tomorrowland first, followed by Buzz Lightyear and possibly Astro Orbiter or the Tomorrowland Speedway. The latter attraction is attractive to kids because it lets them "drive," but it also has the worst queue in Magic Kingdom—guests must stand in the sun, breathing in the noxious exhaust fumes from passing cars. For that reason, if you have children wanting to ride the speedway, try squeezing it in during the morning or evening hours, or nab a rolling FP+ reservation later in the day.

Spending the whole day at Magic Kingdom? Book your FP+ reservations about 60-90 minutes after park opening, so you can get multiple, rolling FastPasses throughout your stay. It's not unheard of for people to get six—or even eight—FP+ reservations by adopting this strategy, though that kind of efficiency won't be realized on peak-crowd days.

If you're hopping to a different park later on, you'll probably want to keep your FP+ reservations for the second park, which will be more crowded by your arrival time, and maximize your rope-drop strategy on the morning of your Magic Kingdom visit. Alternatively, you can book your FP+ selections for Magic Kingdom early on and hope to nab a fourth, rolling FP+ for the second park, understanding you're not likely to get more than that.

Delightful sculptures greet visitors to "the
Hub" section of Magic Kingdom.

## Character Meet-and-Greet Tips

With so many character opportunities spread throughout Magic Kingdom, you'll have to pick and choose which to prioritize. Consult Step Seven for the best character FP+ choices. Meanwhile, here are suggestions to make your interactions as memorable as possible:

- Check the top menu on the MDE app for all character locations. There may be some character meet-and-greets unaccompanied by PhotoPass photographers. To see which are, switch over to the app's "PhotoPass" menu.

- Consider waiting until the end of the day to meet the most popular characters.

- Most kids love having a Disney autograph book on hand for their favorite characters' signatures. But don't let the book get in the way of forging a real connection! Encourage your kids to ask questions and speak freely with the characters, even the ones who can't talk back.

- Liven up your PhotoPass photos by striking a pose. This is especially fun with the more comedic characters.

- If your child is shy, don't force it. Wait and see if the talented cast member portraying the character can draw her out of her shell. If not, know that you may need to wait until your child is older to find the experience worthwhile.

- Fully embrace the experience by bringing your child's Disney princess dress—or other Disney-inspired attire—to wear during meet-and-greets.

## Magic Kingdom for Later Arrivals

If you can't make it to rope drop, your best bet for beating the crowds is to stay late, past the Happily Ever After fireworks show, which usually begins around 9:00pm. Only after the show has ended will guests see drops in attraction wait times, as families with small children begin to depart. If you have plans to see Happily Ever After on another night, it's smart to ride a popular ride during the show itself, when most Walt Disney World visitors will be standing shoulder-to-shoulder on Main Street. You might luck out and see some firework trails while riding Seven Dwarfs Mine Train, Big Thunder Mountain Railroad, or atop Astro Orbiter in Tomorrowland. One neat trick to remember is to get in line for an especially popular attraction about five minutes before Magic Kingdom closes. Disney's cast members will let you ride as long as you've queued up before the top of the hour.

If you have FP+ reservations upon arriving at Magic Kingdom, the best time to use them will be as soon as possible, preferably during the afternoon hours, when wait times mount. Can you bump up an existing FP+ reservation to earlier in the day by hitting "modify" on the MDE app? Check and see. After using all three FP+s, check if any FP+ reservations remain in the system. Aim to get as many rolling FastPasses as you can to bypass longer lines. If FP+ reservations are gone for the day, make it a point to visit some often overlooked attractions, like Carousel of Progress or the Enchanted Tiki Room, or travel by raft over to Tom Sawyer Island, an oasis of tranquility within Magic Kingdom, which many guests love for its caves, forts, and other old-fashioned charms.

# Epcot Rope Drop Procedures and Priorities

Because of its enormous size, a personality split between Future World and World Showcase, and the shared "tiering" of its most popular FP+ attractions, Epcot is a park best toured over two or more days. This is especially true during festival time, when guests will want to slow down and soak in all the ambiance of Epcot's special seasons.

Epcot has two entrances: one in front of the geosphere (the "giant golf ball"), connected to the parking lot, monorail station, and Disney's bus depots, and the International Gateway entrance, used by guests staying at the Epcot resorts and the Swan and Dolphin hotels, or by those folks making the trip from Hollywood Studios. Chances are you'll use the first entrance. The International Gateway approach gives guests riding Frozen Ever After first a slight advantage, since they're both in World Showcase, but the main entrance provides more of a direct shot to the other two rope drop priorities: Test Track and Soarin' Around the World.

Allow ample time for bag check and security at Epcot. This procedure seems to take longer here than at any other park.

Epcot's Future World will typically open at 9:00am on a non-EMH morning, but guests are let through the turnstiles about 30 minutes before the hour and held at various stations inside the park. Because most rides are located in Future World, that's where the majority of people will wait. In fact, World Showcase won't officially open until 11:00am, though guests are allowed back into the Norway pavilion to ride Frozen Ever After at rope drop.

While there isn't an official show to kick off things like there is at Magic Kingdom, an announcement will be made through the park's P.A. system before cast members lead guests toward their first attractions. As is the case in all of Disney's theme parks, running is strictly prohibited. Power walking, on the other hand, is often a matter of survival. Try to be mindful of others, including your children. I've seen parents drag their kids along in a hurry to get somewhere, not conscious enough of their shorter legs. If there's one thing I hate about rope drop, it's the mad rush to be the first one there.

We discussed Epcot's FP+ tiering system and priorities back in Step Seven. You'll probably head to one of three rides at rope drop: Test Track, Soarin' Around the World, or Frozen Ever After. Remember that you can only score a FP+ for one of these attractions, unless you luck out with a rolling FastPass later in the day, a feat much more unlikely at Epcot than it is at Magic Kingdom, at least for Tier One attractions.

What if you have a Park Hopper ticket and are only spending the first half of your day at Epcot, without the benefit of FP+? Head to Frozen Ever After first, come back to Future World to ride Soarin' second, then hit Test Track as a single rider last. Any time left over can be spent experiencing other rides or Future World character meets. Sunshine Seasons in the Land pavilion would make a great lunch stop. World Showcase will have to wait for another day.

The drawback to riding Frozen first is its distance from other Epcot rides. That's why I suggest booking a Frozen FP+

reservation, if possible. Alternatively, if you're planning on spending the entire day at Epcot, you can try slipping into the Frozen line right before park closing, or during the nighttime show, when wait times are lessened.

If you have a Frozen FP+, or don't feel compelled to ride that attraction—and you're not willing to experience Test Track as a single-rider—then you should head to Test Track at rope drop. The line builds quickly for this ride, and will typically see waits in excess of Soarin's. One potential hiccup to bear in mind: Test Track will close due to inclement weather or technical difficulties more than any other Walt Disney World attraction. Visitors to Epcot should keep their schedules flexible for this reason.

It's frustrating when a ride goes down, especially when you have no idea when it may reopen. Keep checking the MDE app's "Wait Times" feature, and filter the park choices for "Epcot." At the bottom of the list are attractions experiencing temporary closures. Keep an eye on this feature, so you won't have to traverse the entire park to see when an attraction has reopened. If you plan on riding Spaceship Earth (note: this attraction is due for a lengthy refurbishment in 2020), the time-travel journey inside Epcot's geosphere, don't make the beginner's blunder of riding it first thing. Because the attraction fronts the park, a lot of Walt Disney World guests will fall into its line as a default. If you don't have a FP+ for Spaceship Earth, wait until leaving the park to ride.

After knocking out the high-priority attractions early in the morning, the afternoon is a great time to slow down and enjoy World Showcase, when most lines in Future World (and Frozen Ever After) max out. Outside of Frozen Ever After and Mexico's Gran Fiesta Tour Starring The Three Caballeros (which rarely sees a wait), there aren't other rides in Epcot's international section, making the afternoon hours ripe for lingering and savoring all the fantastic food, culture, and entertainment at hand. Check the Epcot Times Guide to find out which shows, films, and live-action entertainments are occurring the day of your visit.

And bring your appetite! The World Showcase is the most popular destination for foodies in all of Walt Disney

Epcot's Mission Space is a shuttle simulator
ride that rockets guests to Mars.

World—and for good reason. Even without a scheduled ADR, the quick-service locations and food booths have a bounty of offerings to tempt every palate. If you're looking to relax with an alcoholic drink and a small bite to eat, this is the place to do it.

## Epcot Character Meet-and-Greet Priorities

Here's an important tip to keep in mind at every Disney theme park: pick up a Times Guide as you enter the park for the schedules and locations of all character meets and other entertainment. This is especially important at Epcot, with the park undergoing a two-year, large-scale renovation starting in the fall of 2019, which will have the side affect of displacing popular characters from their meeting spots, to accommodate the new construction.

- **JOY AND SADNESS.** This is a popular meet-and-greet, so try to go first thing in the morning or late in the day, when most guests are visiting World Showcase.
- **MICKEY AND FRIENDS.** Mickey and Goofy will appear temporarily in the Innoventions West building, before finding new homes in the Imagination! Pavilion

(Mickey) and in a venue yet to be determined (Goofy). Minnie Mouse will greet guests in the World Showcase gazebo with Daisy Duck holding court in The American Adventure. Longer wait times without FP+ are possible, as these meet-and-greets enjoy a wide appeal.

- **PRINCESSES IN WORLD SHOWCASE.** There are numerous Disney princesses (and princes) to meet within World Showcase, including Belle in France, Anna and Elsa in Norway, and Snow White in Germany. Lines form quickly.

- **WINNIE THE POOH.** The UK has started hosting a wonderful meet-and-greet with Pooh bear in Christopher Robin's bedroom at the back of the pavilion.

- **EVERYTHING ELSE.** Ralph and Venellope from Wreck-It Ralph meet guests at ImageWorks in the Imagination Pavilion. Meanwhile, keep your eyes peeled when walking around World Showcase. Brief, surprise appearances by Disney characters are more common here than any other place in Disney World.

## Epcot for Later Arrivals

When arriving later to Epcot, it's important to have some FP+ reservations booked, or you'll likely face 1+ hour wait times for Test Track, Soarin', and Frozen. Use Test Track's single-rider capability if you can. If not, get a FP+ for Frozen, gird yourself for riding Soarin' standby, and either put off Test Track for another day, or get into line right before park closing. Wait times peak during the afternoon hours at Epcot, before ticking downward around dinnertime, when many guests are enjoying a meal in World Showcase.

We'll discuss the best spots to view Epcot's interim nightly show, Epcot Forever, in Step Eleven. If you stay to watch the fireworks spectacular, don't rush to beat the crowds out of the park at its conclusion. Guests may enjoy every Disney park for an hour after official park closing. After dark is my favorite time to marvel at the stunning architecture on display in Epcot's World Showcase, and may be yours as well.

# Animal Kingdom Rope Drop Procedures and Priorities

Animal Kingdom is lush, beautiful, and possibly the best themed of all Walt Disney World parks, because of the Imagineers' exquisite attention to detail. It's also the biggest park, though much of that acreage is reserved for the animals, including the savannas guests ride through on Kiliminjaro Safaris. For its size, there aren't a ton of rides to be found at Animal Kingdom, so if rides are your group's priority, the park can be visited in a day. I believe the park is best experienced over two days, however, so that guests can take their time walking the animal trails, soaking up the rich atmosphere, and watching the shows and nighttime entertainment. For children, there are a myriad of educational opportunities to enjoy, with the Wilderness Explorers program being a standout.

Before Pandora opened, rope drop was a fairly simple procedure at Animal Kingdom. After May of 2017, all that changed. It all comes down to one thing: do you have a FP+ reservation for Avatar Flight of Passage or will you ride standby? If you have a FP+, but would like to ride Na'vi River Journey standby, rope drop is fairly straightforward. Arrive at the park entrance about 45 minutes prior to a 9:00 am park opening day. Guests will be let into the park about 30 minutes before the hour, at which point you'll follow the throngs of people heading toward Pandora. Don't worry—most of these guests will head to Flight of Passage. After being let into Pandora about 20 minutes before official park opening (it can vary depending on crowd levels that day), go left to find the Na'vi River Journey entrance and sigh in relief as almost everyone else turns right. If you don't have an Avatar Flight of Passage FP+ booked (and most offsite guests won't), you'll need to do one of three things: 1) arrive 60-80 minutes before park opening and head first to Flight of Passage, 2) get into the attraction's line just before closing, though you could still experience a 1+ hour wait, or 3) ride during the afternoon, when more of Animal Kingdom's crowds have dispersed into other park areas.

It's not pretty, is it? My preference is for option 1, though I understand some might balk at the necessity of showing up that early to ride a single attraction (earlier park openings mean you can show up a little later). The dilemma is that the ride is a knockout, and by showing up even a half hour later for rope drop, you could very possibly see two hours of prime touring time go down the drain. That's how quickly this attraction's line builds—in addition to every other park ride you'll be missing out on because you're stuck waiting for this one. Flight of Passage's wait time rarely drops below 100 minutes all day, though that may change as other theme park lands open up to challenge Pandora's primacy.

What if you aren't hitting Pandora first thing? Good news— things are much simpler for you! Arrive at the park entrance about 20–30 minutes prior to park opening. If you're headed to Asia or DinoLand, you'll be allowed into the park and held beside the Tree of Life. Guests are allowed into the park at 9:00, at which point most guests will make a beeline for Expedition Everest, though some may opt for DINOSAUR. Note that if you're planning on riding Kali River Rapids, you will get wet, making an afternoon ride preferable on most days. For this reason, Kali is often a great use of FP+, especially in the summer months.

If you're visiting Africa first, you'll be taken to a different location near the Pizzafari restaurant, and admitted at 9:00.

Animal Kingdom's Expedition Everest towers into
the night sky behind the Rivers of Light venue.

Kilimanjaro Safaris is my pick for a first ride over every other, non-Pandora attraction. The animals are a little more active during the cooler hours, and the line for Kilimanjaro Safaris is routinely longer than Expedition Everest or DINOSAUR later in the day. Guests will often ride Kilimanjaro first, before heading over to ride Expedition Everest. At that time of day, it's possible to ride Everest multiple times before a significant line builds.

If you're spending the entire day at Animal Kingdom, keep checking the MDE app for any Na'vi River Journey or Flight of Passage FP+s that might drop into the system due to cancellations. It does happen, on occasion, especially for Na'vi. Otherwise, it's probably not as essential for rope droppers to hunt for a rolling FastPass at Animal Kingdom, since so much can be accomplished during the early hours. Remember Expedition Everest's single-rider line, if needed. Grabbing a Rivers of Light FP+ as your fourth pick would be a good get if you're planning on staying for the nighttime show and haven't purchased a dining package.

Your afternoon plans for Animal Kingdom might include some wildlife time on the Gorilla Falls, Discovery Island, and Maharaja Jungle Trek trails. If you begin to overheat (and Animal Kingdom will definitely take a toll on its guests in the summer), cool off in an air-conditioned theater to watch Festival of the Lion King or Finding Nemo. The former, especially, blows guests away with its Broadway-caliber theatrics.

## Animal Kingdom for Later Arrivals

Similar to rope drop, the Pandora attractions present the biggest hurdle for guests arriving later in the day to Animal Kingdom. Hopefully, you'll have a FP+ reservation for either Avatar Flight of Passage or Na'vi River Journey. Whichever attraction you can't use FP+ for, do one of two things: 1) ride between 1 and 5 pm or 2) get into line right before park closing. The Na'vi River Journey line shouldn't be too bad at night, and to be frank, a lot of guests don't think this attraction is worth more than a 30-minute wait. It's a beautiful visual experience, but somewhat slight from a storytelling standpoint.

Otherwise, your non-Pandora FP+ reservations should be set for the afternoon, when park lines are longest. It's unlikely that late-arriving guests will secure any meaningful rolling FastPasses, especially during busier weeks of the year, but it never hurts to check the MDE app for availability, especially if you're hoping to secure a FP+ for Rivers of Light. Again, bear in mind that outside of Pandora's attractions, Kiliminjaro Safaris and Kali River Rapids (on hot days) will present the longest waits, followed by Expedition Everest and DINOSAUR. Make sure to ride Kali at the hottest time of day, when you may not mind having a wet shirt and drippy socks. (Disney provides free lockers near Kali to store a change of clothes, if necessary.)

Only one Animal Kingdom character encounter offers FP+: Mickey and Minnie at Adventurers Outpost. This is a fantastic interaction that shouldn't be missed. On average, guests may wait 30 minutes, so it's not a terrible use of FP+, especially for the youngest members of your party. Animal Kingdom has the fewest character meet-and-greets of any Disney World park, and none of the others require a substantial investment of time.

Whatever your arrival time to Animal Kingdom, make sure to visit Pandora after dark, when the bioluminescence from the floating mountains and plant life imbues the land with an otherworldly glow, evoking awe and wonder in onlookers. I'm also an enormous fan of the Tree of Life's Awakenings show, which plays from dark until park closing. This stunning visual projection on the Tree of Life is filled with beautiful, delicate moments. In fact, it might be my favorite thing to observe in all of Animal Kingdom.

# Hollywood Studios Rope Drop Procedures and Priorities

The force is strong with Disney's Hollywood Studios—as is fan interest in Galaxy's Edge, the Star Wars land opening to rave reviews, and waves of crowds, in late August 2019. Coming on the heels of Toy Story Land's successful debut in 2018, Hollywood Studios has quickly become Orlando's hottest ticket, which may excite or intimidate guests planning a visit.

**STAR WARS**: Because the park's operating times and procedures are fluid for the foreseeable future, Hollywood Studios touring strategies should be taken with a Death Star-sized grain of salt, at least until both Star Wars attractions are opened and FastPass+ allocation seems set. Currently, Disney is handling Galaxy's Edge's oversized appeal by permitting Disney resort guests to enjoy extended morning Extra Magic Hours throughout the park. They're also reducing FastPass efficiency by piling most of the desirable attractions into Tier One, so as to keep guests occupied outside the new land. FastPass+ availability for Millennium Falcon: Smuggler's Run and Rise of the Resistance (opening December 5, 2019) is not available at print time, though may be soon. Check the Disney website for updates.

What's the bottom line to all this? If you're eager to experience Galaxy's Edge's immersive theming, cutting-edge attractions, fanciful eateries and souvenir outposts, I'd set aside two days (or two half days, when in possession of a Park Hopper ticket) for Hollywood Studios: one for Star Wars, and another for everything else. If you're a Disney resort guest, take maximum advantage of Extra Magic Hours to get your Star Wars fill. If staying offsite, opt for a late-night visit on an evening without Extra Magic Hours—though you may not be able to build a custom-designed light saber at Savi's Workshop or grab a drink from Oga's Cantina, since both locations are low-capacity venues that will field increasing demand throughout the day.

For guests rope dropping Galaxy's Edge on a non-EMH day, arrive at least 90 minutes before park opening and head straight for Oga's Cantina or Savi's Workshop if those are must-do experiences for your party. If not, plan on riding Rise of the Resistance or Millennium Falcon: Smuggler's Run initially. Because you can only experience one Star Wars attraction at a time, it's likely you'll face a lengthy wait for whichever ride you elect to do second. Be sure to download the Play Disney Parks app to entertain yourself in line. There is a lot to excite and engage Galaxy's Edge guests within this mobile platform.

Luckily, Galaxy's Edge—like Pandora in Disney's Animal Kingdom—was imagineered to be an experience tailored to individuals' interests and passions, rather than just a couple of rides to check off a list. Take the time to absorb all the jaw-dropping details that make up the planet of Batuu—and the remote village of Black Spire Outpost—and actively engage with the Disney cast members who play their parts of traders, adventurers and smugglers to the hilt. After all, this is the closest many of us will ever get to being a part of a galaxy that, as kids, we could only dream about.

**THE REST OF THE PARK**: For guests prioritizing the rest of Hollywood Studios, arriving 45 minutes before park opening (typically at 9:00 am) should suffice. Parents of a 4–12 year-old eager to take part in Jedi Training Academy (see Step 12) should head straight for the registration area at rope drop, before moving on to your first attraction. Ask a Disney cast member for the location of the sign-up.

It will behoove you to book your FastPasses early at Hollywood Studios, if hoping to acquire additional, Tier One FastPasses throughout your day. In fact, I'd consider booking a low-priority, third FastPass, such as Muppet Vision 3D, to successfully stack your morning FastPasses, availing yourself of possible Slinky Dog Dash, Tower of Terror and/or Rock 'n' Roller Coaster FastPasses later on. Note: you can check into a "throwaway" FastPass+ touch point of any attraction and walk out if you're more interested in booking a fourth, high-priority FastPass than experiencing the "lesser" attraction. (But for the record: I love MuppetVision.)

Once Mickey and Minnie's Runaway Railway opens in early 2020, it will likely become most guests' FastPass+ priority, if the two Star Wars attractions still lack an FP+ option, or are in a separate tier. Without FastPass+ access to Mickey and Minnie's railway adventure, I'd head for this attraction right at park opening, to avoid lengthy waits later on.

For folks making Toy Story Land their rope-drop priority, head to Slinky Dog Dash Roller Coaster first. Those with a desire to meet Woody, Jessie, and Buzz Lightyear should stop by the meet-and-greet after disembarking Slinky Dog, before taking a turn on Toy Story Mania or Alien Swirling Saucers. Then it could be time for your first FastPass+ attraction, followed by a second and third, if utilizing the rolling FastPass+ strategy discussed above.

If nobody in your party is interested in Hollywood Studios' more intense rides, you may not be as focused on securing

It's always fun watching Stormtroopers interact with guests visiting Disney's Hollywood Studios.

rolling FastPasses. The rest of your morning could pass quite agreeably and may include a number of attractive character options, such as meeting Olaf near Echo Lake and the Disney Junior Pals in Animation Courtyard—or Mickey and Minnie on Commissary Lane—capped off by the use of FP+ at the Frozen Sing-Along Celebration. The other shows' FP+ option isn't necessary, but Frozen's special seating can save time.

If staying to watch Fantasmic! later on, you can try to nab a rolling FastPass for the nighttime show. Without FP+, you'll need to arrive 60–90 minutes before showtime to secure a good seat.

It's nearly impossible to watch Fantasmic! and any other Hollywood Studios nighttime spectacular on the same evening, unless there's a second Fantasmic! scheduled that night. Keep this in mind when deciding how many days to visit Hollywood Studios, and whether a Park Hopper ticket might not come in handy for this reason, and for Galaxy's Edge.

Afternoons can be spent enjoying the park's stage shows and the Star Wars Launch Bay, as you'll want to a) avoid the rides' longest lines and b) cool off during the hottest parts of the day. Make sure you grab a Times Guide to see when the stage shows begin, including the start times for the various Star Wars entertainments. This is another challenging part to touring Hollywood Studios efficiently: it's difficult to hit all the shows in a single day, and doing so requires a lot of back-and-forth. This is why it's best to look through the "Entertainment" section on the Disney website, filter it for Hollywood Studios, and include those shows you hope to watch in your My Disney Experience plans. Write down the start times you're aiming for, and take a copy of those plans into the park. It's not a bad idea to look at a park map beforehand, too, if you're trying to figure out the most efficient order in which to see the shows to minimize the wear on your legs.

## Hollywood Studios for Later Arrivals

If you're headed to Hollywood Studios later in the day, it's essential to have FP+ reservations booked when visiting lands outside of Galaxy's Edge. Otherwise, you'll be setting yourself up for frustration. And if you're hoping to take advantage of evening Extra Magic Hours to experience decreased attraction wait times, it rarely works in this park. In fact, I'd go so far as to avoid Hollywood Studios on evenings with EMH, unless your focus is Star Wars.

As was the case in other parks, late arrivers should book FP+ reservations in the afternoon, when lines are longest. Rolling FastPass+ availability may be slim at this time. Except at peak-crowd times of the year, wait times for character meet-and-greets and most attractions will drop after dinner. If you're looking to avoid the heat during an afternoon visit to Hollywood Studios, head to the Star Wars Launch Bay or to the Frozen Sing-Along Celebration, Voyage of the Little Mermaid, or Muppet*Vision 3D, all of which come with a welcome blast of air conditioning. Walt Disney Presents is an engaging exhibit to walk through when escaping the heat—or a sudden, torrential downpour—and has a lot to offer Walt Disney and Mickey Mouse nostalgists, in addition to previewing a bevy of exciting changes in store for Disney's films and theme parks.

Guests interested in saving time in the Rock 'n' Roller Coaster queue can head to the single-rider line, or alternatively, make it the last ride of your day, minutes before park closing. Slinky Dog Dash will show reduced wait times just before closing, too. Hitting Toy Story Mania, Tower of Terror, and Rock 'n' Roller Coaster may be doable for guests wanting to maximize the final 1–2 hours of park time, as other Hollywood Studios visitors begin to stake out spots in advance of the nighttime shows, or find themselves absorbing Galaxy Edge's after-dark delights.

If your focus is meet-and-greets, in lieu of attractions, visit those characters you're most excited about during the last hour of their scheduled appearances to minimize your waits.

# The Wonderful World of Baby Care Centers

If you have a child under five at Walt Disney World, be sure to acquaint yourself with each park's Baby Care Center, a wonderful oasis of quiet, air conditioning, and copious baby supplies. Each center is equipped with:

- Changing tables
- A unisex bathroom
- A private nursing room with rocking chairs
- Highchairs
- A kitchen with a microwave, oven, and sink
- Sofas for relaxation
- A shop offering formula, baby food, juice, diapers, wipes, sunscreen, and OTC medications and clothes for purchase

# Last Word

Sometimes things don't go according to plan. Kids balk at riding attractions, or don't want to meet that one character you were absolutely certain they'd love. Maybe your daughter didn't sleep well the night before and decides to have a melt-down on Main Street, U.S.A. Or someone in your party isn't feeling well and needs to go back to the resort early, spoiling your plans for dinner that evening.

*Nobody* has the perfect Walt Disney World vacation. There are simply too many balls in the air to keep from dropping some. Be kind to yourself if you hit a stumbling block, and remember that it's not your responsibility to make everyone happy. If you have to change your itinerary, change it, and try not to hold onto any disappointment you might feel in the aftermath. There will be more opportunities to enjoy tomorrow—and if you love Walt Disney World as much as I do, you'll always be looking for a reason to come back.

# Lining Up Entertainment in the Parks

Nobody puts on a show like Disney. From its first forays into animation, the Walt Disney Company has harnessed story-telling magic, technological innovation, and creative talent to bring magic to millions, expanding its reach in 1955 with the opening of Disneyland, a theme park designed to take families on a fantastical journey to another world. Walt Disney himself once remarked, "It's kind of fun to do the impossible." And when you experience a nighttime show at Walt Disney World, you feel the truth of that statement with all of your senses.

It's not just the big nighttime spectaculars that capture the imagination of Disney World visitors. That Disney touch extends to the resort's most intimate venues and off-the-cuff interactions with cast members. It's my intention in this chapter to highlight the best entertainment experiences at Walt Disney World—big *and* small, so guests can plan for the most popular shows, while embracing unexpected opportunities as well.

Because I touched on the parks' stage shows in the last chapter, I'll omit them here, but you should check all the entertainment options (and start times) on Disney's website, including numerous worthy entries I didn't have space to accommodate in this chapter. Be sure to double-check the information as your trip dates draw near, as Disney is constantly shaking up its entertainment lineup, or pick up a Times Guide at the park that day.

# Magic Kingdom

## Happily Ever After

Magic Kingdom's new nighttime spectacular, and my number-one pick for "must-do" show at Walt Disney World. Watch in wonder as Cinderella Castle is transformed into a magical canvas for the animated highlights of your favorite Disney films, topped off by heart-pounding fireworks and a soaring musical score. This is a stunning show for guests of all ages and a fitting way to close out an unforgettable day at the world's favorite theme park.

**DURATION:** 18 minutes.

**WHERE TO WATCH.** Because the show relies heavily on castle projections, it's best to watch it on Main Street, U.S.A. My favorite spot is near the hub, the grassy area in front of the castle. Some people like to watch farther back—with the hope of making a quick exit afterward—but I think you lose something with the buildings of Main Street infringing on your view.

**WHEN TO FIND A SPOT:** Happily Ever After will usually start around 9:00 pm. For the best locations, line up 60–90 minutes beforehand, depending on crowd conditions that day.

**HINTS:** Stand in front of a trash can, or the fence surrounding the grassy hub, so other guests can't block your view.

**EXTRAS:** Kick up your fireworks excitement by indulging in one of three Happily Ever After dessert parties: two before the show and one right after.

**HOLIDAY SUBSTITUTIONS:** In an effort to make the holidays as memorable as possible, Disney will showcase special fireworks shows in lieu of Happily Ever After. Celebrate America: A Fourth of July Concert in the Sky is held on July 3 and 4. Halloween fireworks are shown exclusively on Mickey's NotSo-Scary Halloween Party nights. Guests can catch Holiday Wishes when attending Mickey's Very Merry Christmas Party, or during regular park showings in the week around Christmas. Finally, there's the Fantasy in the Sky fireworks to ring in the new year, shown twice on December 30 and 31.

## The Festival of Fantasy Parade

A daily opportunity for Disney World guests to see their favorite Disney heroes' and villains' stories brought to life in a succession of floats accompanied by a memorable soundtrack, capped off by a heart-stopping appearance by Sleeping Beauty's fire-breathing dragon, Maleficent.

**DURATION:** About 12 minutes.

**WHERE TO WATCH:** The best spot to view the parade, and for photos, is on Main Street. If you'd rather not invest the time in reserving a spot here, good vantage points can be found in both Liberty Square and Frontierland, where the parade starts.

**WHEN TO FIND A SPOT:** FFor the best locations on Main Street: 60 minutes. Anywhere else: 30–45 minutes.

**HINTS:** IIf you have a DSLR camera, the characters on the floats will often make a special point of waving to you. Keep your camera in "burst" mode.

**EXTRAS:** Guests may purchase a Tony's Town Square Dining Package, with VIP seating for the parade.

**HOLIDAY SUBSTITUTIONS:** Walt Disney World will substitute Mickey's Once Upon a Christmastime Parade for Festival of Fantasy during Christmas week.

## "The Muppets Presents...Great Moments in American History"

The historical puppet comedy you never knew you needed. Join Kermit the Frog, Miss Piggy, and all your favorite Muppets as they narrate familiar stories of our nation's founding with all the humor, music, and pathos you'd expect from this bunch of madcap pranksters. Performed 8–10 times on most days.

**DURATION:** 10 minutes.

**WHERE TO WATCH:** Liberty Square, near the Hall of Presidents. The Muppets appear in the windows of the Heritage House.

**WHEN TO FIND A SPOT:** Whenever you feel like it!

**HINTS:** There are two versions of the show; try to catch both.

## Mickey's Royal Friendship Faire

This show unrolls the red carpet at Cinderella Castle five times a day, affording Walt Disney World guests the chance to see their favorite Disney characters join forces in a lively celebration of music, dance, and unrivaled pageantry. Mickey and Goofy are there, along with beloved characters from *Tangled*, *The Princess and the Frog*, and *Frozen*.

**DURATION:** 23 minutes.

**WHERE TO WATCH:** In front of the *Partners* statue of Mickey and Walt Disney.

**WHEN TO FIND A SPOT:** A few minutes prior to showtime.

**HINTS:** See an earlier show in case of afternoon thunderstorms.

## Main Street Shows

Treasure the old-fashioned charm of Main Street, U.S.A. while taking in one of several musical performances showcased there throughout the day. Older guests will savor nostalgic musical gems brought to life by the Dapper Dans and the Main Street Trolley Show. Guests young and old will tap their feet to the popping beats of the Main Street Philharmonic Band. Finally, veterans are honored every day near dusk in a somber, but uplifting Flag Retreat ceremony.

**DURATION:** 15–20 minutes for all performances.

**WHERE TO WATCH:** For the Flag Retreat, near the flagpole. Otherwise, the performers will pass down Main Street.

**WHEN TO FIND A SPOT:** Check the Times Guide for showtimes.

**HINTS:** While none of these shows is a "must do," it's worth lingering on Main Street long enough to catch at least one. The cast members are friendly and charismatic, and the iconic location only enhances their charms.

**EXTRAS:** If you have a veteran in your traveling party whom you'd like to honor, go to City Hall first thing in the morning to ask that he be selected to participate in Flag Retreat that day. Only one veteran per day is chosen.

# Epcot

## Epcot Forever

Epcot bid farewell to the long-running IllumiNations in the fall of 2019, ushering in its new interim show, Epcot Forever, that will run for about a year before being replaced by a permanent, nighttime spectacular set to cap off that park's massive, multi-year overhaul. For Epcot nostalgists, the temporary show is sure to stir hearts and unlock memories, as it features fire-works, lasers and special-effect "kites" choreographed to iconic tunes from the park's storied past. While the show promises to be a beautiful visual spectacle to all onlookers, it will take on extra dimension for Epcot loyalists for whom the mention of "Horizons" can still put a tear in their eye.

**DURATION:** 15 minutes.

**WHERE TO WATCH:** World Showcase is full of good options for nighttime viewing. First, though: if you want to leave the park via Future World immediately following the show's conclusion, you should watch from World Showcase Plaza at the northern end of the lagoon (between the two gift shops). Other optimal locations are La Cantina de San Angel

Epcot's Tokyo Dining terrace offers a wonderful
vantage point to watch the fireworks.

restaurant, the bridge between the U.K. and France, the area between Norway and Mexico, the Italian gondola landing, and the second-floor terrace outside of Tokyo Dining (you don't have to eat there to enjoy the show).

**WHEN TO FIND A SPOT:** For prime locations such as World Showcase Plaza, expect to line up 60 minutes before showtime. To eat at La Cantina de San Angel, find a table 90 minutes in advance. For other locations, 30–45 minutes may suffice.

**HINTS:** There are numerous trees and lampposts that can hinder guests' views of the show, so make sure to stake out a clear vista. Also, if you're racing to beat the crowds out of the park once the show ends, make sure to hold fast to your child's hand.

**EXTRAS:** There will likely be a FP+ reserved viewing option for Epcot Forever, but with so many good vantage points found throughout World Showcase, it likely won't be necessary. For a pricier, seated option, consider the dessert party instead

## Serveur Amusant

A delightful stop in any family's World Showcase tour. While remarkable expressions of talent and culture can be enjoyed throughout every nation's Epcot pavilion, none leaves onlookers as routinely amazed as this two-person troupe that combines elegant acrobatics with sly, cutting humor. Gets as many laughs as gasps in its five daily showings.

**DURATION:** 20 minutes.

**WHERE TO WATCH:** Near Les Chefs de France in France.

**WHEN TO FIND A SPOT:** Check a Times Guide. For all of the street-side performances in World Showcase, you can show up when you want, and leave when you've had enough.

## Voices of Liberty

This 8-person *a cappella* group performs much-beloved tunes from the American folk and patriotic songbooks. Attired in 18th-century costumes, the singers' arrangements and harmonies are flawless, and their execution of these timeless classics are stirring to guests young and old.

**DURATION:** 15 minutes.

**WHERE TO WATCH:** In the rotunda of the American Adventure.

**WHEN TO FIND A SPOT:** Check the Epcot Times Guide.

**HINTS:** Take a seat in the air-conditioned rotunda and enjoy this show on a balmy Epcot day.

# Animal Kingdom

## Rivers of Light: We Are One

A different kind of Walt Disney World nighttime spectacular that harnesses the magic of light, water, and sound to take guests on a mystical journey celebrating the ancient bonds between man and nature. The show enjoys a lush, lagoon setting, with seated guests marveling at brightly lit floats and giant water screens that feature a stunning array of animals, all brought to life by the river's "shamans." In 2019, characters from Disney's animated films were included to deepen guests' engagement with the story. Whatever your level of enthusiasm for a fireworks-less nighttime show, the artistry of the experience can't be denied. Check if two shows are being offered on the night you plan on attending.

**DURATION:** 15 minutes, after an extended pre-show.

**WHERE TO WATCH:** In the amphitheater between Asia and DinoLand. The best seats are found in the middle. There is also a standing-room only area at the back, in case you have a restless child with whom you need to make an early exit.

**WHEN TO FIND A SPOT:** If using the standby entrance, start lining up 30–60 minutes prior to showtime, depending on crowd levels that day. For the FP+ and Dining Package entrance, 15–30 minutes before showtime should suffice.

**HINTS:** If there's a second showing of Rivers of Light on the night you attend, see that one. If you're only spending one day at Animal Kingdom— and there's but one show of Rivers of Light—think hard about whether you'd rather see the show or visit Pandora at night. My vote would be for Pandora.

**EXTRAS:** Guests may secure FP+ seating for Rivers of Light. This is a fine use of FP+ since it will save you time in the standby line. However, I'd probably try to get it as a rolling FP+, and not use Rivers of Light as one of my first three FP+ selections at Animal Kingdom. For guests on the Disney Dining Plan (or for those people willing to pay out-of-pocket), reserving a dining package for the show, in conjunction with a meal at Tusker House, is an excellent use of a table-service credit, as the voucher you'll receive guarantees priority seating. You can also opt for the fine-dining route, using two table-service credits at Tiffins. Additionally, there is a dessert party available for guests to book in advance.

## Tree of Life Awakenings

This gorgeous projection show takes place after sunset on Animal Kingdom nights, running continuously through park closing. Watch the multitude of animals on the Tree of Life come alive in a series of small vignettes that leaves a big smile on the face of Walt Disney World onlookers. It's one of my favorite experiences in all the four theme parks—both for the beauty of its special effects and for the ease with which you can stand there and watch these delicate stories take flight.

**DURATION:** 10–15 minutes, then the "awakening" repeats.

**WHERE TO WATCH:** In front of the Tree of Life on Discovery Island

**WHEN TO FIND A SPOT:** Any time.

**HINTS:** If you're a photographer with a tripod, long-exposure shots here can yield interesting results.

## DiVine

The remarkable street performer whom Animal Kingdom visitors might be forgiven for thinking is a tree! Brought to life by performance artist Priscilla Blight—graceful on her stilts even while festooned in foliage—DiVine emerges slowly from the forest around her, startling the visitors passing by and teaching us all about the powers of observation while being immersed in nature.

**DURATION:** 20 minutes.

**WHERE TO WATCH:** Usually in the Oasis, but sometimes on the trail between Africa and Asia. Ask a cast member where she'll be appearing that day.

**WHEN TO FIND A SPOT:** Any time you hear the leaves rustle or see a tree move.

*Note*: Animal Kingdom features a variety of fantastic musical acts which can be found by checking the Times Guide on the day of your visit, or just enjoyed while passing by. Whether it's the thrilling rhythms of the Tam Tam Drummers of Harambe in Africa or the joyous, Indian dancing demonstrated by Asia's Bollywood Beats, you're sure to find something that gets your heart pumping and your feet moving. Performances can be enjoyed multiple times a day, so keep your ears open!

# Hollywood Studios

## Fantasmic!

The most theatrical of the Walt Disney World nighttime shows, featuring an epic battle between good and evil. On one side is Mickey Mouse, reprising his role as the Sorcerer's Apprentice from *Fantasia*, and championing the power of imagination with the help of classic Disney heroes and heroines. On the other side is the Wicked Queen from *Snow White*, marshaling the nightmarish menace of Disney's most notorious villains in order to vanquish Mickey and his friends once and for all. Dramatic lighting, fireworks, water projections, and thunderous music combine to make this a spellbinding show for the thousands of onlookers in the Hollywood Hills Amphitheater each night.

**DURATION:** 30 minutes.

**WHERE TO WATCH:** Hollywood Hills Amphitheater. Follow the path to the right of the Tower of Terror and make your way back.

**WHEN TO FIND A SPOT:** Early. Though the amphitheater is enormous, the show is packed on most nights. For standby seating, arrive at least 60 minutes prior to showtime. (For a second showing, 50 minutes should suffice.) For FP+ entry, you should still get there 30–45 minutes early. For dining package voucher seating, 30 minutes should suffice.

**HINTS:** This is an intense show for young kids, so decide ahead of time whether you think your child can handle it by checking out a YouTube clip. If there are two shows on the night you plan on visiting, see the second performance for fewer guests.

**EXTRAS:** FP+ is available for Fantasmic!, though I would only grab one as a rolling FP+ selection, as guests with FP+ still have to arrive quite early to secure a good seat. The better option, especially for guests on the table-service Dining Plan, is to reserve a Fantasmic! Dining Package, either for Hollywood & Vine, Hollywood Brown Derby, or Mama Melrose's Risotrante Italiano. If Fantasmic! is cancelled on the night you'd planned on attending, you'll receive a voucher good for another performance in the next 7 days, so schedule your dining package near the beginning of your trip if weather is a concern.

## Star Wars: A Galactic Spectacular

The epic nighttime show every Star Wars fan will want to see at least once while visiting Hollywood Studios. Utilizing projection technology, fireworks, lasers, and shooting flames—all choreographed to the iconic music of John Williams' score—guests are thrust into storylines they know by heart, but made to feel anew. This is a thrilling show to watch for even the casual Star Wars devotee and one of Walt Disney World's most popular nighttime entertainments.

The Tam Tam Drummers of Harambe will
enliven any Animal Kingdom visit.

**DURATION:** 14 minutes.

**WHERE TO WATCH:** There are multiple vantage points from which to watch Star Wars: A Galactic Spectacular, but because the film projections on the Chinese Theater are so integral to the story, the best spot is right on Hollywood Boulevard, a few hundred feet back from the theater. If you stand too far back on Hollywood (past the Sunset Boulevard intersection), the buildings will block out the fireworks. If you choose a spot near Echo Lake, you'll see the fireworks, but not the projections.

**WHEN TO FIND A SPOT:** Stake out a spot 30–45 minutes before the show and hope nobody taller slips in front.

**HINTS:** Most of the fireworks are shot off to the right, so stand slightly to the left when facing the theater.

**EXTRAS:** There isn't a dining package or FP+ associated with this one. Instead, guests may reserve a spot at the Star Wars: A Galactic Spectacular dessert party.

**HOLIDAY SUBSTITUTIONS:** For the last few years, Hollywood Studios' guests have enjoyed the holiday hijinks of Jingle Bell, Jingle BAM! in lieu of Star Wars: A Galactic Spectacular, until the final two weeks of the holiday season, at which time both productions are shown at night, in addition to Fantasmic!

# Adding Extras Your Family Will Love

There's so much to do on a Walt Disney World vacation that it can be difficult to get everything in, especially for first-time visitors. But that doesn't mean you can't make room in your itinerary for some one-of-a-kind experiences, too. If you or a loved one will be celebrating a birthday, anniversary, or other special occasion while visiting Walt Disney World—or simply want to take that extra step to make a trip unforgettable— consider incorporating one or more of Disney's Enchanting Extras into your plans. While the expense of such add-ons can seem prohibitive, Disney includes a range of choices for the budget-minded traveler, too, including experiences sure to strike a chord in the heart of every adventure-loving kid.

In this chapter, I'll highlight the most appealing Disney trip enhancements, starting with many that are completely free and ending with some that, well, aren't.

## Free

**HIDDEN MICKEYS.** If it seems like you keep bumping into Mickey Mouse while visiting the Walt Disney World resort— that's by design! The Disney Imagineers enjoy slipping the iconic shape of Mickey's head everywhere they can think of, from the lock on the jail cell in the Pirates of the Caribbean attraction to the flagstone floor of the Polynesian. In doing so, they've created a fun challenge designed to pique their guests' powers of observation. Try to find Hidden Mickeys during your Disney World stay.

**SORCERERS OF THE MAGIC KINGDOM.** This is a free scavenger-hunt style game open to all Magic Kingdom guests. What's the goal? Participants must stop Hades—and a cohort of evil Disney villains—from taking over Magic Kingdom by apprenticing themselves to Merlin the magician. After signing up for the game at the firehouse on Main Street, U.S.A., new enrollees are given a mystical map to 20 magic portals throughout the theme park, a pack of spell cards to defeat the villains, and a Sorcerer Key Card to unlock the first portal, revealing a secret mission. Each quest takes 20–30 minutes to play, with nine challenges in all. The best part? Apprentices receive a pack of new spell cards with every visit made to Magic Kingdom. Many participants enjoy trading these cards—which make for a great collector's item—with fellow players within the park.

**CELEBRATION BUTTON.** If someone in your party is marking a special occasion during her vacation, like a birthday, anniversary, honeymoon, or even a first visit to Disney World, stop at any Guest Relations window, Disney resort desk, or Magic Kingdom's City Hall to pick up a celebration button to wear that day. Disney's cast members make it a point of showering celebrating guests with special attention, and the buttons make for a nice souvenir of your stay. Also—and this is no guarantee!—some birthday button-wearers have been known to score a free dessert while dining at Disney's table-service restaurants.

**AGENT P'S WORLD SHOWCASE ADVENTURE.** *Phineas & Ferb* was an animated show about two boys with a pet platypus named Perry who was also a secret agent charged with preventing a megalomaniacal doctor from taking over the world. In Epcot, guests can sign up for a game channeling Agent P's exploits as they leave Future World for World Showcase. (Look for the Agent P signs on your left.) Using their smartphones, and by downloading the Disney Parks Play app, enlisted visitors help Agent P solve clues to defeat Dr. Doofenshmirtz in one of seven World Showcase pavilions. Each game takes about 30 minutes to complete, and can be a great way of keeping younger kids invested in World Showcase, where attention sometimes flags. (If it's raining the day of your visit, pick Mexico for your mission, as all the clues are hidden inside the pavilion.

**KIDCOT FUN STOPS**. This is another way of keeping children engaged in the culturally rich, but less attraction-focused, World Showcase. Each pavilion boasts a Kidcot stop, staffed by Disney cast members native to that country, who will chat with your child as he collects a souvenir fact card and colors a scene on the other side. If you have an outgoing child eager to learn a few words in another language—or who simply loves coloring—Kidcot is a great way of letting him have fun while you catch a break. Stop at as few—or as many—Kidcot stops as you like. They're open from 11:00 am each day.

**WILDERNESS EXPLORERS**. Of all the free, interactive adventures for Walt Disney World families to enjoy, Wilderness Explorers is the best of the bunch, especially for 5–12 year-olds. Inspired by the Pixar film Up, in which Russell and his faithful dog Dug set out to explore the world, your child can earn more than 30 wilderness explorer badges by completing tasks scattered throughout Animal Kingdom. These fun, conservation-themed challenges range from learning that flamingos aren't really pink to digging for "fossils" and distinguishing various animal calls. Disney's cast members are experts at interacting with kids of all ages and temperaments, and kids get a big kick out of leading their parents around on a mission that's also educational. Each child achieves a rank based on total tasks completed, but garnering all 33 could take the entire day! Fortunately, you can return to your wilderness challenge across multiple Animal Kingdom visits. If interested in Wilderness Explorers, pick up a field guide at any station. Most guests start their adventures at headquarters, on the bridge between the Oasis and Discovery Island.

**JEDI TRAINING ACADEMY.** Young Padawans aged 4–12 years of age may test their lightsaber skills against the Dark Side villains of the epic Star Wars saga when visiting Hollywood Studios. Parental sign-up is required and should be completed early on to ensure your child is enrolled in one of the dozen daily time slots. Note: At press time, it is not known whether Jedi Training Academy will continue to be hosted on the stage near Star Tours, or be moved inside Galaxy's Edge.

# Budget Options

**EPCOT WORLD SHOWCASE PASSPORT KIT ($12.99).** A cheap, easy way to enrich any World Showcase visit. Guests may purchase a passport kit from most Epcot stores, which includes a passport, World Showcase pin, and a set of colorful stickers reflecting points of interest throughout Epcot's countries. As you stroll around the pavilions, your child can attach stickers to the appropriate landmarks. Make sure to stop by the pavilion's Kidcot location to get the passport stamped. The cast members there will often write something special—or draw a picture—inside the pages to personalize it.

**PIN TRADING (~$20).** Collecting Disney pins is a popular hobby among Walt Disney World enthusiasts, and can be a relatively cheap way to have fun and interact with cast members. The key is to buy the pins before a trip. On Amazon or eBay, you may purchase 25 pins for $20, while in the parks, a single pin will run you $9. So, if you think you or your child might be interested in starting a pin collection (and to be official, pins must bear the

Walt Disney World's cast members are what make programs like Animal Kingdom's Wilderness Explorers shine.

©Disney mark), buy them now to take on vacation later. The cheaper "lot" pins may not be the most desirable, but that's the magic of pin trading. When you get to the parks, and see a cast member wearing a lanyard full of shiny hardware, ask politely to see their pins. If you see one you like, offer a trade. You'll soon be embarking on an exciting new collection.

**AUTOGRAPH BOOK (~$8).** For Disney World guests anticipating a lot of character interactions, buying an autograph book is a great way to ensure you have a personalized souvenir, filled with magical memories, to take home later.

**HARMONY BARBER SHOP HAIRCUT ($18–$25).** Anyone may make an appointment at Magic Kingdom's Harmony Barber Shop on Main Street, U.S.A., though the most popular offering at this charming establishment is the My First Haircut package designed for the tiniest Walt Disney World guests. For little more than the cost of some Mickey ears, your child will get a certificate commemorating his experience, a lock of hair to take home, and the aforementioned Mickey ears with "My First Haircut" embroidered on the back. Don't worry if your baby's hair isn't that long yet. The experience is worth more than the haircut itself, and the barbers do an excellent job of keeping young children entertained. Not a bad deal for $25! Kids' haircuts are $18; an adult haircut runs $19. Although not an official service advertised by Harmony Barber Shop, guests can get their hair styled in a braid, bun, or mohawk with a sprinkling of "pixie dust" (large, colorful glitter) for $5. This is a great, inexpensive alternative to the more extravagant Bibbidi Bobbidi Boutique treatment discussed later. If you didn't make a reservation in advance, stop by in the morning to ask if they can squeeze you in that day.

**BIKE RENTALS ($18–$25).** Many Disney World resorts rent bikes for individual or group use, which can be a fun, relaxing way of spending some quality family time outside of the parks. Traditional bicycles are available; some locations also offer Surrey bikes—vehicles seating anywhere from 2–6 people. Surrey bikes are an especially common sight near the Epcot resorts and BoardWalk area. Rentals typically last 30 minutes. Check your resort's recreation options to see where bikes are available.

**BEHIND THE SEEDS TOUR ($25).** Walt Disney World offers a bounty of special tours and behind-the-scene experiences for your education and enjoyment. While many tours can be cost-prohibitive, a few are highly affordable while still drawing rave reviews. If you or a travel partner has a passion for gardening or the natural sciences, this one-hour Epcot tour of their four greenhouses and fish farm is a goldmine of information and potential interest. To reserve a spot, call (407) WDW-TOUR up to 180 days in advance.

**CARING FOR GIANTS / UP CLOSE WITH RHINOS TOURS ($30 / $40).** Likewise, for those Walt Disney World guests with an abiding love for wildlife, here is a relatively inexpensive way of getting an intimate, up-close look at the elephants and rhinos that call Animal Kingdom home. Learn about the complex social bonds connecting these gentle giants, and what it takes to keep them healthy and happy in a theme park setting. On this hour-long tour, you'll also have the chance to take photos and find out what you can do to aid conservation efforts back on their native continent. Offered multiple times across most Animal Kingdom days. Call (407) WDW-TOUR for a reservation.

# Moderate Options

**CAKE DELIVERY TO A RESTAURANT OR RESORT ($35+).** To surprise a loved one with a celebratory cake at a special meal, add this option to your dining reservation by calling (407) WDW-DINE at least 72 hours in advance. Alternatively, you may have a cake delivered to a Disney resort room by dialing (407) 827-2253. A range of cake styles and messages are available. For an assortment of cake, gift basket, and other floral arrangement options, visit http://disneyworld. disneyfloralandgifts.com.

**CARRIAGE RIDE ($55 FOR 4-5 PEOPLE).** Escape into the quiet, wooded acreage of Fort Wilderness, or enjoy the southern charms of Port Orleans Riverside as you're transported by horse-drawn carriage along the peaceful Sassagoula River. Each carriage holds four adults, or two adults and three small children, for an excursion lasting 25 minutes. Call (407) WDW-PLAY up to 180 days out for a reservation.

Disney's Port Orleans Riverside Resort conjures up a
romantic backdrop for an evening carriage ride.

**DINING PACKAGE ($39–$74/ADULT, $18–35/CHILD).** Guests
may reserve dining packages for Magic Kingdom's Festival of
Fantasy Parade, Hollywood Studios' Fantasmic!, or Animal
Kingdom's Rivers of Light and Festival of the Lion King shows,
which guarantee special seating access to the entertainment
after enjoying a meal at one of seven Disney restaurants. (Prices
vary per restaurant.) Dining packages are an especially cost-effective option for Disney Dining Plan purchasers, since many
packages can be "bought" for the price of a single table-service
credit. Call (407) WDW-DINE to make reservations, and inform
the Disney cast member if you're on the Dining Plan.

**THE PIRATES LEAGUE ($19.95–$44.95+/PACKAGE).** For children 3 years of age and up with a flair for the dramatic, the
Pirates League in Magic Kingdom may be the perfect outlet for
channeling their inner thespian. Kids may choose to be transformed into either a pirate, Captain Hook, or a zombie, all while
being regaled by high tales of sunken ships and buried treasure
from Disney's attentive cast members. Each child is bestowed
a unique name reflecting his new identity and, as a final flour-
ish, will be initiated into the Pirates League at the end of his

sitting. Reservations are available 180 days in advance of your visit and can be made on the Disney website. To get the most out of the experience, schedule an early appointment.

# Splurges

**DESSERT PARTY ($69–$84/ADULT, $41–$50/CHILD).** We touched on dessert parties in previous chapters, and how party guests may sample a wide variety of specially themed Disney desserts while enjoying VIP seating at the four theme parks' nightly shows. I find dessert parties to be of questionable value for a typical family's vacation budget. (When it comes right down to it, how many cupcakes can one person eat?) Sure, dessert parties will save you some stress in finding a good fireworks viewing spot, but at a fairly hefty cost. That said, they're an increasingly popular splurge for Walt Disney World guests, so there is likely value to be found here. If I had to recommend one, it'd be the Star Wars Galactic Spectacular Dessert Party, but only for the serious Star Wars fan. Dessert party reservations are typically released later than other dining reservations, so keep your eye peeled to Disney's website for updated info. To save money on the Fireworks Dessert Party at Magic Kingdom, book the Plaza Garden View option. You'll stand for the fireworks, but from a better vantage point than the costlier Tomorrowland Terrace Dessert Party (though people with mobility issues will appreciate the seating there).

**BIBBIDI BOBBIDI BOUTIQUE ($74.95–$450/PRINCESS, $19.95–$79.95/KNIGHT).** Bibbidi Bobbidi Boutique is a special experience for kids, and one of the most popular splurges to be had at Disney World. If you have an excited Disney princess fan in your life, this is the way to make all her dreams come true. Following a turn at the salon, where she'll be given an elegant up-do, girls are treated to manicures, makeup, costumes, and special royal accessories (dependent on the specific package; see Disney's website for details). Boys get in on the fun with the help of some hair gel and knightly accoutrements. Makeovers take 30–60 minutes. Photo packages may be purchased, but aren't necessary for guests with Memory Maker. Reservations can be made online in advance, starting at 180 days out. Bibbidi Bobbidi Boutique is also available at the Disney Springs Marketplace and Disney's Grand Floridian Resort & Spa. Schedule Bibbidi Bobbidi Boutique early on, and make a stop at her favorite character meet-and-greet afterward for a very special photo op.

**PIRATES & PALS FIREWORKS VOYAGE ($75/ADULT, $45/ CHILD).** For a fireworks experience designed to be memorable, I give the nod to The Pirates & Pals Fireworks Voyage. The night starts out at Disney's Contemporary Resort, with a small scavenger hunt and a photo-friendly visit from Mr. Smee and Captain Hook. Snacks and desserts are plentiful in the fun, pirate-themed setting, until a wisecracking pirate named Patch accompanies guests down to the Contemporary's dock, where they'll be launched by boat into the Seven Seas Lagoon, enjoying songs, games, and general hijinks until the fireworks begin. After taking in the sights and sounds of Happily Ever After, the boat heads back to the Contemporary, where the star of the evening—Peter Pan—awaits guests young and old. While the vantage may not be ideal for seeing the Cinderella Castle projections, the experience as a whole is richer and more rewarding than any dessert party. Boats are ECV/wheelchair accessible. For the best fireworks viewing, request the odd-numbered rows on the boat. Reserve a spot through Disney's website.

**FIREWORKS CRUISE (STARTING AT $299/BOAT ACCOMMO-DATING 10 GUESTS).** If you're looking for a more intimate way of savoring a special occasion than sharing a boat with tiny pirates, you might book a specialty cruise by calling (407) WDW-PLAY up to 180 days in advance of a trip. A range of different vessels—from a 10-person pontoon up to an elegant, 18-person grand yacht—can accommodate most parties, casting off from docks around the Magic Kingdom and Epcot resorts. Enjoy snacks and tasteful decorations as you drift along the Seven Seas Lagoon or Crescent Lake, and watch the Happily Ever After or Epcot Forever fireworks explode in the night sky to reflect in the surrounding waters. To make your celebration truly memorable, request private dining and/or butler service at booking. The romantic possibilities are endless.

**HALLOWEEN AND CHRISTMAS PARTIES ($79–$139/ADULT, $74–$134/CHILD).** As discussed in previous chapters, guests can immerse themselves in Disney's holiday magic with the help of two ticketed Magic Kingdom events: Mickey's Not-SoScary Halloween Party and Mickey's Very Merry Christmas Party. The former is offered on select nights beginning in late August and ending a few days after Halloween, with the Christmas party launching shortly afterward and concluding just before Christmas. Ticket prices rise as the holiday in question draws near, and it's to guests' advantage to purchase tickets in advance (you do not need regular park admission when attending a party only). While guests may enter the park as early as 4pm, the parties don't officially start until 7pm, at which point guests can expect to enjoy holiday parades and stage shows, character meet-and-greets, snacks (including Halloween trick-or-treating), and shortened attraction wait times, capped off by a special fireworks display, before things wrap up at midnight. These are pricey events, and if I were to pick one, I'd choose Mickey's Not-So-Scary Halloween Party, which has a bit more to offer guests, especially to those arriving in costume. I would not attend a party with young children who might struggle to stay up late or who don't yet have the patience for the more extensive character-meet lines. The parties are popular events, so don't walk into Magic Kingdom expecting the park to be empty.

**EARLY MORNING MAGIC ($79/ADULT, $69/CHILD).** One of the best ways of getting a jumpstart on your Magic Kingdom visit is to purchase an advance ticket for the Early Morning Magic experience, offered select Tuesdays and Sundays in the Fantasyland section of the park (check Disney's website for dates). For the price of the ticket (and regular park admission), guests may enjoy unlimited rides on 6 Fantasyland attractions, including the very popular Seven Dwarfs Mine Train and Peter Pan's Flight, from 7:45 until the park's opening at 9:00, before indulging in a delicious breakfast buffet at Cosmic Ray's Starlight Cafe, from 9:00-10:00. This event may be worth it for some families, particularly those with younger kids on a shorter-length stay. You'll get enough food to fill your belly until mid-afternoon and the chance to ride two of Walt Disney World's most popular attractions as many times as you want! Plus, there's something truly wonderful about having the park almost to yourself, especially when that means avoiding lines later. Note: The future of Disney's Hollywood Studios' Early Morning Magic is uncertain at this book's publication, but in the past has granted guests access to the Toy Story Land attractions, along with breakfast, for $79/adult, and $69/child.

**AFTER HOUR ($125–$144/PERSON).** Did you ever wish you could have Disney's Animal Kingdom, Hollywood Studios or the Magic Kingdom all to yourself? Well, now's your chance to make that dream come true—very nearly! The "After Hours" events enable ticketed guests to enter a chosen park at 7 pm, though the real fun doesn't begin until 9-10, after the parks have been closed to regular visitors. That's when attraction wait times plummet, as After Hours guests breeze through popular rides and character meet-and-greets in record time, all while enjoying unlimited Mickey bars, popcorn and bottled beverages, and soaking up the late-night atmosphere unique to each park. These events might be pricey, but I've yet to hear a single, lukewarm response from those participating. If I had

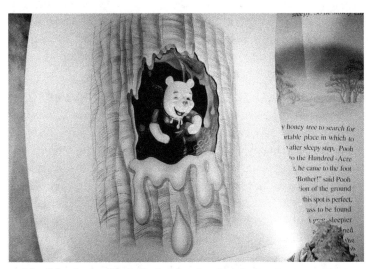

Like Winnie the Pooh, Early Morning Magic guests can expect some sweet surprises at Cosmic Ray's Starlight Cafe.

to pick one, I'd choose Magic Kingdom, since that park hosts the most attractions. After Hours tickets can be booked online or by calling (407) 939-7795. Buying ahead is smart to secure a discount, and to ensure tickets don't sell out. Regular park admission is not required.

**TOURS ($49–$275/PERSON).** Disney offers an array of longer-length tours for guests eager to take a peek at the behind-the-scenes magic inside Walt Disney World's theme parks and resorts. These experiences may be especially appealing to Disney enthusiasts, animal lovers, or for guests booking longer vacations who foresee ample opportunities for greater exploration. For a closer look at specific tour offerings, along with their price points, check out the "Events and Tours" link under "Things To Do" on Disney's website. One of the most popular offerings is Disney's Keys to the Kingdom, a 5-hour walking tour of Magic Kingdom, which includes fascinating trivia about Walt Disney and his magnificent park, special access to Disney's famed Utilidor tunnels, and a delicious lunch. Guests agree that Disney's cast members are what make these tours shine. This is especially true of the Wild Africa Trek at Disney's Animal Kingdom, a thrilling 3-hour tour that rounds out the wonder of the natural world with amazing facts and stories from the animal guides. The expedition even includes a walk across a suspended rope bridge! To book a tour, call (407) WDWTOUR up to 180 days in advance. Be sure to check the physical requirements in each tour's description before reserving.

**VICTORIA & ALBERT'S DINNER ($185–$400/PERSON).** Consistently regarded by Walt Disney World enthusiasts as one of their favorite splurges, a meal at the world-famous Victoria & Albert's at Disney's Grand Floridian is a dining experience worth savoring. Guests at this renowned restaurant can look forward to exquisite pairings of modern American cuisine with artfully selected wine. Attention to detail and meticulous service combine to lift the occasion from ordinary to exceptional. Choose one of three formal dining spaces and menus, ranging from 7 courses in the elegant main Dining Room to the exclusive 13-course meal served at the intimate Chef's Table. While I'd be hard-pressed to spend this much money on a single meal, true foodies may consider a dinner at Victoria & Albert's to be the crown jewel of their Walt Disney World stay. For Dining Room and Queen Victoria Room reservations, guests may book online 180 days in advance of their meal (or earlier for guests staying at a Disney resort). For dining at Chef's Table, phone (407) WDW-DVNA in advance.

**SENSES SPA (PRICES VARY WITH PACKAGE CHOSEN: $35– $475).** For the ultimate in indulgence, call (407) WDW-SPAS to make an appointment at Senses, the Disney spa found at Wilderness Lodge and Saratoga Springs. Touring the Walt Disney World theme parks can take a physical toll on a person. So why not set aside a couple of hours for a relaxing massage? Body wraps, manicures and pedicures, facials, hydrotherapy, and a host of other pampering options can be enjoyed singly or together, in one of many packages offered to individuals and couples. Kids can get in on the action when accompanied by an adult.

# Planning for Fun Outside the Parks

If you're fortunate enough to enjoy an extended vacation at Walt Disney World, I suggest setting aside a day or two to spend outside of the four major theme parks. While it may be tempting to "get your money's worth" by riding every ride, meeting every character, and seeing every show Disney offers within its parks, for vacations lasting more than five days, there's ample opportunity to slow down and explore the rich diversity of experiences Disney World extends to its visitors. You might even surprise yourself and find that these "down" days are among the most memorable of your vacation, because they don't require the stringent planning a theme park visit often entails. For most of the destinations in this chapter, you can simply show up and enjoy yourself. And what could be better than that?

In this section, we'll discuss the shopping, entertainment, and culinary delights found at Disney Springs and Disney's BoardWalk, the best approach for visiting the spectacularly themed Walt Disney World resorts, and the water park and golfing fun available to guests who just can't help but stay active.

A note to guests booking shorter Walt Disney World stays: you may still be able to explore one or more of these destinations, without sacrificing a full day of your vacation. Arrival and departure days are ideal opportunities to visit less popular Disney locales. Or, you may find you have a few hours left over after a theme park visit, and want something beyond pool time to look forward to.

# Disney Springs

If you enjoy good food and shopping, and the chance to unwind with quality entertainment, beat a path to Disney Springs to explore the outdoor, waterside promenade attracting more and more Walt Disney World guests by the day. Formerly known as Downtown Disney, the district was reimagined in 2015, opening to rave reviews and renewed interest from visitors eager to sample the rich assortment of restaurants and shops located in four Disney Springs sectors: West Side, Town Center, the Landing, and Marketplace. Buses travel to Disney Springs from all Disney resorts, and from the theme parks after 4pm. (They do not run from Disney Springs back to the theme parks.) Boat service runs to and from Disney Springs via Old Key West, Saratoga Springs, and the two Port Orleans resorts. For drivers, it's simple: complimentary parking can be found at its parking garages.

## Disney Springs Entertainment

In addition to featuring a rich assortment of restaurants and stores, the Disney Springs area also boasts an AMC Theater and a retro, upscale bowling alley called Splitsville that's a lot of fun for large groups and families. In 2019, Disney Springs opened its doors to NBA Experience, a huge complex hosting state-of-the-art, immersive games and competitions for guests eager to throw themselves into the basketball action of their dreams.

Because Disney Springs is an outdoor venue, be sure to check the weather report before visiting. Bring rain gear when necessary, and wear comfortable shoes, as there is a lot of walking. During summer, it's smart to visit Disney Springs early in the day, before temperatures peak and restaurants get crowded. That's the time to come with young kids, who will love taking a spin on the Marketplace's carousel or train, followed by a refreshing run through the splash pad.

For a soaring view of the Walt Disney World resort, including the theme parks, splurge on an Aerophile tethered balloon ride ($20/adult, $15/child), lifting off multiple times a day between West Side and the Landing. Boat rides and Italian water taxi tours are also available, but for those looking to burn a little more money ($125), why not take a cruise of the Disney Springs area in a chauffeured Amphicar, the only land-water vehicle of its kind in the world. If free is more your style, have fun posing for a PhotoPass photo with the world-famous Coca-Cola bear at the Coca-Cola store, before heading up for a rooftop view of the surrounding area. For Disney World guests who've purchased Memory Maker in advance, stop by the PhotoPass Studio at the Marketplace for individual or group portrait sessions with an impressive array of Disney backgrounds, no reservation required.

While musical and other artistic performances occur throughout the day at multiple Disney Springs locations, to truly enjoy all the energy and excitement the venue brings to bear, guests should visit after sundown, when the bright lights and live music electrify the walkways. Whether it's Irish dancing at Raglan Road, or a chart-topping musical act enjoyed with a bowl of jambalaya at the iconic House of Blues, Disney Springs vibrates at night with stage and street performances, all attracting a youthful, vibrant clientele.

## Dining at Disney Springs

Because there's such a quantity of fantastic eating options at Disney Springs, I'll refrain from making personal recommendations here. Be sure to check out the "Dining" section of Disney's website and filter for "Disney Springs" at the top of the page to call up menus for individual eateries. For most table-service restaurants, you'll need to secure an advance dining reservation via the MDE website or app. If you're unable to find an ADR for the restaurant you want, check opentable.com, another online restaurant reservation system for select Disney Springs restaurants. Don't forget to mention that you're a Disney Visa holder or Annual Passholder to your server when dining: many Disney Springs restaurants—as well as shops—offer discounts.

## Shopping at Disney Springs

For the most unique shopping Disney Springs offers, head to the Marketplace. That's where you'll find the 50,000 square-foot World of Disney store, along with two destinations kids go nuts for: Once Upon A Toy and the LEGO store. For

Disney items targeted toward collectors and enthusiasts, don't miss the Art of Disney, Disney's Days of Christmas, and the Marketplace Co-Op, which features one-of-a-kind clothes, accessories, and home furnishings. The Marketplace is also home to Disney Springs' version of Bibbidi Bobbidi Boutique, discussed in Step Twelve.

Town Center is where you'll find a less Disney-centric selection of boutiques and stores, featuring recognizable brands such as Kate Spade, Lacoste, Sephora, Under Armour, and Vera Bradley. Walking around Town Center feels akin to a shopping experience at any other upscale, outdoor mall you might find in a big city, which makes it a little less interesting to me. That said, the Japanese retailer UNIQLO is a great place to stop for Disney-inspired clothing you can buy for less than what you'd pay at the theme parks.

The Ganachery, located in the Landing, is a must-stop for the family chocoholic. Visitors can watch the chocolatiers whip up delicious, Disney-inspired treats and chocolate bars, before deciding on which indulgence(s) to take home. Standout retail locations in the West Side of Disney Springs include a

When hunting for vacation souvenirs, shoppers won't find a better selection of items than World of Disney's.

soccer-centric store called Pelé Soccer, Star Wars Galactic Outpost, Superhero Headquarters, and Harley Davidson.

*Note*: At most Disney Springs shops, guests may request their purchases be taken to the Disney Springs Welcome Center for later pick-up, which is a nice convenience.

# Disney's BoardWalk

As much as I appreciate the wealth of offerings at Disney Springs, there's just something about Disney's BoardWalk that speaks to the romantic in me. Inspired by the bustling 1920's boardwalk cities of Atlantic City and Coney Island, this waterside destination—just a short hop and a skip from Epcot's International Gateway—evokes a palpable nostalgia with its glittering dance hall, lively street performances, delightful shops, midway games, and tasty eateries. It's also small enough to not overwhelm, and thus a perfect place to land after a busy day spent touring Epcot or Hollywood Studios.

Guests can take a short walk from Epcot, the Epcot resorts and the Skyliner station to the BoardWalk, or a slightly longer one via the path from Hollywood Studios. Friendship boat service is also available from all Crescent Lake locations. If traveling from another Disney destination, hop aboard a BoardWalk Inn bus and, upon arriving, walk through that resort's lobby to reach the BoardWalk on the other side. Drivers will have a tougher go of it, as the BoardWalk Inn parking attendants don't always allow non-resort guests to park in its lot, especially during busier times of the year. Valet parking is available for $33, or guests can choose to take a rideshare service or taxi.

Entertainment highlights at Disney's BoardWalk include the Atlantic Dance Hall, open Tuesdays through Saturdays, from 9pm to 2am, to guests 21 years and up who relish a spin on the dance floor. Jellyrolls, with nightly hours from 7pm to 2am, would be my top pick for the 21-and-up set, though. This rollicking bar features dueling piano players and lively audience singalongs, though all that fun comes with a $15 cover charge. If there's someone in your party who can't bear to miss the big game, head to the ESPN Club, where he's bound to find something he likes on one of 100+ television screens, all while enjoying a beer and some bar food. For guests desiring more upscale fare, you can't do better than booking an ADR at Flying Fish, the BoardWalk's premier, fine-dining restaurant. A bit of time before your ADR? Duck into the enchanting AbracadaBar for a magical cocktail in this illusionist's paradise.

For couples and families who desire an after-dinner stroll, jugglers, street musicians, and other performers entertain Thursday through Saturday evenings to give the BoardWalk the feel of an authentic street festival. Caricature artists and hair wrappers also offer their services. And don't forget the Surrey Bike Rentals I mentioned back in Step Twelve if you want a fun way of burning off the calories you imbibed at Ample Hills Creamery, a delicious ice cream shop with a turn-of-the-century charm. There are BoardWalk shops for browsing or shopping, and for the kids, arcade and carnival games where they can spend their parents' money.

Disney's BoardWalk is a destination on the rise, especially for guests who have the luxury of spending a week or more at Walt Disney World.

# Blizzard Beach & Typhoon Lagoon

If we let our daughter decide what to do on any given day of a Walt Disney World vacation, she's liable to pick a water park. While this used to surprise me, I'm beginning to understand her logic. After all, there's no early-morning rope drop to make at a water park, which typically opens at 10am. While there are still lines to endure, they're nothing like the waits at the four major theme parks, and there's always a wave pool or lazy river to enjoy when things get hectic. Disney's water parks are as impeccably themed as the four major theme parks, while the waterslides serve up a ton of fun. And no matter how hot it is on an Orlando afternoon in July, that water is always going to feel cool and refreshing against your skin.

So it's a no-brainer to get a Park Hopper Plus Ticket (see Step Three) for Disney World vacations lasting five days or longer during the warmer months of the year. Trust me—if you have kids, they'll love you for the upgrade. There's just no reason to pay a $69 single water park admission ($63/child) when you can get multiple water park, golfing, and minia-ture-golf admissions with a Park Hopper Plus ticket for less money than the price of a single entry.

When picking which day to visit Blizzard Beach or Typhoon Lagoon in winter, keep a lookout for the warmest day in the forecast, and go then. The water is heated at both parks, but it can still get chilly. Check the Disney website to see which water park is open to guests, as one typically closes during the cold season. And when traveling during the warmer months, don't be scared off by the possibility of showers. While guests aren't allowed on attractions during a thunderstorm, downpours are usually short-lived and can clear the park of other visitors. Do try to arrive at the water parks right at park opening, so you can claim the shaded lounge chairs and ride the more popular attractions while the parks enjoy minimal crowds. Attendance typically spikes mid-afternoon. Cabana rentals are available for a hefty fee— reserve by calling (407) WDW-PLAY.

If you're allotting one day of your Disney vacation to water park fun, and can't decide which one to visit, here is my advice: If you have young kids or a couple daredevils in your group, go to Blizzard Beach. The Ski Patrol Training Camp is wonderful for youngsters, while Slush Gusher and Summit Plummet offer plenty of thrills for teens and adrenaline junkies. But if you're a beach bum at heart who wants your water park to have that laid-back vibe, pack your sunscreen and head to Typhoon Lagoon, which has a fantastic family raft ride, wave pool, and lazy river.

Guests catch bus transportation to both water parks from their resorts. Some have a single bus stop designated for water park transfers. Buses may stop at multiple Disney resorts to pick up other guests. You cannot catch a bus from the theme parks to a water park. Traveling by car? You'll be happy to hear that parking is free at both destinations. Guests should wear their waterproof MagicBands when heading out for a water park day. There are PhotoPass opportunities at Blizzard Beach and Typhoon Lagoon, which is especially valuable in locations where you're less likely to have a camera handy.

Towels are available for a small fee at both water parks, while locker rentals cost $10 (small) or $15 (large) per day. Life

To get the complete putt-putt experience,
golfers should play both the "summer" and
"winter" sides at Disney's Winter Summerland.

jackets are free. Don't forget to bring water shoes, as the pave-
ment can get blistering. For guests bringing food to the parks,
picnic tables are available—but don't bring glass or alcohol.
Dining choices are mostly limited to standard, theme-park
fare, though my husband and I have been pleasantly surprised
by our meals at Typhoon Lagoon's Leaning Palms. If you eat
nothing else at either place, though, you have to try their
famed mini donuts (coated in powdered sugar and paired with
your choice of dipping sauce); they are warm and delectable.

# Fantasia Gardens & Winter Summerland Miniature Golf

Another reason to upgrade a Park Hopper ticket to a Park Hopper Plus is the ability to play miniature golf at both Fantasia Gardens and Winter Summerland, without paying the $14 admission fee ($12/child) at each stop. The only hitch is you'll need to start a game before 4pm when using a "Plus Visit" from your Park Hopper Plus ticket, and guests may not play both courses on the same day. Standard operating hours are from 10am to 10pm, though Fantasia Gardens often stays open until 11pm.

Our kids love spending an hour or two miniature golfing each trip. It's a fun way to unwind and spend some quality family time together. Our favorite course to visit is Winter Summerland, which has two sides—Winter and Summer—with admission covering play on the side of your choice. This whimsical course is a little easier than Fantasia Gardens. In fact, for young kids, Fantasia Gardens may present too great a putt-putt challenge. In hot weather, Winter Summerland will be the better option for everyone, as it has more shade and is adjacent to Blizzard Beach, making it a convenient stop after a water park outing.

It's simpler to get to Winter Summerland via Disney bus transportation because guests can just board a bus bound for Blizzard Beach. Make sure you're done golfing by 5pm if the water park closes early, though, so you can catch a bus back to your resort. Parking is free if driving.

To access Fantasia Gardens, either hop on a bus headed to Hollywood Studios and walk the 0.7 miles to the miniature golf course, or take a bus bound for the Swan hotel, which will bring you closer to your destination. Fantasia Gardens parking is free.

# Golf

Golfers on a Walt Disney World vacation are in luck: the resort boasts three championship golf courses (par 72) plus the nine-hole Oak Trail walking course ideal for beginners and families. Of the three full-length courses, Lake Buena Vista offers that classic, country club feel, prizing accuracy over power inside its narrow greens. The Magnolia Golf Course is dotted with challenging water hazards, sand traps (one in the shape of a Mickey head), and the clear vistas that come with long, open fairways. Disney's Palm Golf Course is peaceful, if prickly: the course is riddled with an abundance of trees and includes nine water holes to up the difficulty factor.

If you're a Disney resort guest, contact Bell Services the night before your tee time to receive a taxi voucher for transportation to the course, in addition to arranging for a pick-up time. Tee times are reserved by calling (407) WDW-GOLF up to 90 days in advance for Disney resort guests, or 60 days for offsite guests. Walkups may be accommodated. For guests in possession of a Park Hopper Plus ticket, a round of golf at Oak Tree counts as a "Plus Visit." If you need to cancel your tee time, do so 48 hours before your reservation to avoid a penalty. Golf cart, club, and shoe rentals are available at all courses, and private instruction may be arranged.

# Disney Resort Hopping

Resort hopping is a rewarding way to spend a full or half day of an extended vacation, especially during the holidays, when Christmas decorations adorn the already dazzling Disney resorts. A typical resort hopper might start with the resorts connected by the Magic Kingdom's monorail line: the Contemporary, the Polynesian, and the Grand Floridian. Another possibility is to take the boat over to Wilderness Lodge and/or the nearby Fort Wilderness campgrounds from the Magic Kingdom dock. Guests won't need a dining reservation to explore these properties, though you can always stop at a lounge or bar to pick up a drink or snack. There is no swimming at other resorts' pools, however.

For Epcot resort hoppers, take the International Gateway entrance at the back of World Showcase to have a look around the BoardWalk Inn, Beach Club, and Yacht Club Resorts; they're also just a Friendship boat or Skyliner ride away from Hollywood Studios. Bus transportation is available to Moderate and Value resort guests, too, as long as you bear in mind that there is no bus service between Disney resorts—meaning you must return to the theme park you started from to find transport back to your own accommodations. For this reason, resort hopping can often take longer than envisioned.

Disney resorts are also accessible by car. Just inform the security guard at the resort parking gate that you'd like to have a look around. It helps to be a Disney resort guest when asking, especially when hopping to the most popular Deluxe resorts, where parking is tightly regulated, particularly during peak travel seasons. Another way of ensuring access is to schedule an ADR for a resort restaurant, or tell the parking attendant you want to eat at the counter-service location inside. When all else fails, there's drop-off via taxi and rideshare services, and valet parking for a fee.

For guests resort hopping to Disney's Art of Animation resort, drawing classes are offered daily.

Here are some special events you might plan a visit to a Disney resort around:

- **GRAND FLORIDIAN RESORT & SPA.** There is no lovelier spot in all of Walt Disney World to sit and unwind than the lobby of the Grand Floridian Resort, especially when the Grand Floridian Society Orchestra is entertaining guests with their lively mix of ragtime, Dixie, jazz and Disney classics. Grab a drink or snack and settle in for one of several delightful performance across the resort's late afternoon and evening hours.

- **POLYNESIAN VILLAGE RESORT.** Evening is an ideal time to tour the popular Polynesian Resort. Adults will want to visit Trader Sam's Grog Grotto, a themed Tiki bar bursting with Disney details, while also serving up inspired food and drinks. If it's busy inside, grab a refreshing Dole Whip treat from Aloha Isle instead. For families, there's nothing better than heading to the Poly's beach after dark to watch the Magic Kingdom fireworks and the Electrical Water Pageant, a Disney World tradition since 1971. See the brightly lit King Triton lead his assortment of sea monsters, whales, turtles, and other denizens across the Seven Seas Lagoon. The parade swings by the Polynesian at 9:00pm most nights.

- **FORT WILDERNESS CAMPGROUNDS.** For an experience like none other at Disney World, grab your cowboy boots and mosey on over to Fort Wilderness, the backcountry retreat replete with wooded scenery, native wildlife, a host of recreational activities, and even a horse ranch. If vacationing during the holidays, check out out the creative Christmas decorations that pop up on the visiting RVs and tents from campers who return to Fort Wilderness annually. Be sure to pop in for the Chip 'N' Dale Campfire Sing-Along before departing in the evening. Magic Kingdom's fireworks and the Electrical Water Pageant can both be viewed from the beach area. A word of warning, though: Fort Wilderness is huge, so be prepared to walk or use the property's internal bus system for getting around.

- **ANIMAL KINGDOM LODGE.** The Animal Kingdom Lodge offers public viewing areas of its savannah animals, which both guests and visitors to the resort may enjoy. The best time to visit is during feeding, around 5pm each day. As a bonus, ask a cast member at the lobby counter for an Animal Viewing Guide to assist you.

- **PORT ORLEANS RIVERSIDE.** This is a serene, pictur-esque resort to visit during the daytime hours, but if you make it over to Port Orleans Riverside on most Wednesday through Saturday evenings after 8:30pm, stop by the River Roost Lounge Bar to see a beloved Disney performer tickle the ivories—and light up guests' faces—during a fantastic three-set show. "Yeeha" Bob Jackson has been a celebrated piano player, singer, and cutup comedian at Port Orleans since 1997, and his act remains fresh and fun to this day. As a bonus option, take the 10-minute walk over to Riverside's sister resort, Port Orleans French Quarter, to sample its delicious beignets.

- **ART OF ANIMATION.** This is my favorite Value resort to visit because of its movie-rich, larger-than-life theming, starting with the beautiful Animation Hall that first greets Disney guests checking in. When exploring Art of Animation, see if a drawing class is being offered that day in the lobby for the wannabe Disney animator in your party. Lessons are normally held at 11am, 2pm, and 5pm. Art of Animation also hosts a Skyliner stop with its sister resort, Pop Century, for guests wanting to travel by gondola to Hollywood Studios and Epcot.

Resort hopping is a great way of getting the full flavor of Walt Disney World—and a smart way of scouting out future accommodations for that next trip to Orlando!

# Packing for Your Trip

The countdown keeps dropping and the excitement is building: it's almost time for your Walt Disney World vacation!

Before traveling to Orlando, let's make sure you have everything you need to make your trip a success. Your packing list may differ from the lists offered here—after all, you're the one who understands your travel habits best. My job is to help you think of items that aren't necessarily on your vacation radar, especially for a first-time trip to Disney World. That doesn't mean you should take everything mentioned in this chapter! In fact, I will happily attest that our family makes it a point of packing lightly for our Orlando trips. But if you're the kind of person who wants to feel prepared for every eventuality, feel free to use these lists as a starting guide, and build from there.

The first factor to consider when packing for Walt Disney World is the weather awaiting you in Orlando. In the days leading up to your vacation, check the forecast often. Remember to look at the high and low temperatures—while 56 degrees may seem warm to a family enduring a Minnesota blizzard mid-January, it will feel quite chilly when racing around Big Thunder Mountain at night. Dressing in layers is smart practice for wintertime Disney World vacationers. In summertime, stick to lightweight fabrics. Instead of denim shorts, opt for cotton or the wicking fabrics found in athletic wear. Trust me—the less weight on you the better. That includes what you carry into the parks.

That brings us to bags. Now that our children are older, we've found we like going "bagless" on our theme park days, because it cuts out the necessity of going through "bag check" lines at security and keeps us less bogged down throughout the day. How do we accomplish this miraculous feat? Cargo shorts and pockets, mainly. Between my husband and myself, we carry our phones, a collapsible water bottle, credit cards and ID, a small tube of sunscreen, wet wipes, pain medication, and a phone charger. If it's hot, and the kids and I want to bring cooling towels into the parks, we'll wrap them around our necks. If rain's expected, we'll grab cheap, disposable rain ponchos, still in their packaging. And with two teenagers, that's all we really need to get by. But for parents of younger children, a park bag is almost always a necessity.

Be mindful of how much walking Walt Disney World demands of its guests when deciding on a park bag. During the summer, it's essential to keep the extra weight off your body. Find a lightweight bag you can store conveniently beneath a stroller or sling across your body. While a fanny pack might seem like a questionable fashion choice, your shoulders will thank you for sacrificing vanity for practicality. If requiring something larger, I prefer a gender-neutral, crossbody bag, with plenty of compartments and pockets, to a bulkier backpack. That way, if you're traveling with your spouse or significant other, you can share the responsibility for carrying your belongings. And make sure you include an ID tag somewhere on the bag with your cell number, in case it's misplaced. Here are my suggestions for possible items to include in your theme park day bag, remembering that if you think you can live without it—you probably can.

# Theme Park Bag

- MagicBands or hard tickets
- printouts of FP+ reservations and ADRs
- park maps and Times Guides
- driver's license/ID, credit cards, insurance card, Disney gift cards, cash
- water bottle
- small sunscreen
- lip balm with sunscreen
- sunglasses with strap

- hat/visor
- hand sanitizer/Wet Wipes
- quarters and pennies for penny-pressing machines
- hair ties
- small hairbrush
- sweater/jacket/sweatshirt
- phone
- portable battery charger
- camera with extra battery
- change of clothes for kids (after splash pad fun, water rides, or accidents)
- dry socks (after rain or water rides)
- large Ziploc bags for separating items and keeping them dry
- food/snacks
- a towel to set on the ground before parades
- Disney pins
- autograph book with thick-barreled pen
- tissues
- Ibuprofen
- Band-aids
- Moleskin for blisters
- cooling towels (i.e., Frogg Togg)
- water-mister fan
- ponchos or umbrella
- glow sticks/wands/necklaces for kids before fireworks
- gum (Disney doesn't sell it)
- baby needs (bottles, food, sippy cup, pacifiers, bibs, diapers, wipes)
- water park essentials (swimsuit, towel, goggles, water shoes)

Try to pare down this list to meet your most essential needs. In the meantime, here are further factors to prepare for ahead of your time in the parks:

- Protect your feet. Prevent blisters by breaking in a pair of comfortable walking shoes before the trip (no heels or flip-flops). Pack Body Glide or foot powder in your suitcase, if necessary. Bring insoles for extra cushioning and Moleskin (plus a pair of small scissors) to prevent chafing should blisters develop.

- Consider your camera needs. Is your smartphone enough, or is a point-and-shoot more your style? And what about the gold standard for photography—a DSLR? If you're a skilled photographer, taking your DSLR (or renting one) will be tempting. A word of caution: even if your camera and lens don't feel heavy now, they'll feel like an albatross around your neck at the end of a long Disney day. You may also need backup batteries and memory cards. If you want to take fireworks photos, a small, collapsible tripod and a remote shutter release cord will be helpful. DSLR photography can sometimes slow the pace of a family vacation. The results might be worth it to you, but what about the people you're traveling with? Can you make do with PhotoPass and Memory Maker instead?

- Charge your phone the night before a theme park visit and bring a portable battery charger into the parks, if needed. Disney sells FuelRods at charging kiosks, but you'll spend less bringing one from home.

- When bringing food into the parks, coolers may not exceed 24" x 15" x 18". Soft, insulated ones work best. If you need to store food before a mealtime, Disney rents lockers to guests. Strollers also make handy storage vehicles. Microwaves for warming food can be found at Disney's Baby Care centers. Counter-service restaurants provide free cups of water or ice. If you want to keep your water bottle and other drinks cool, freeze them the night before. Pack snacks that are easy to eat on the go. And finally: no glass containers or alcohol are allowed inside the parks.

- Think about securing an ID tag to your younger child's clothing or shoes, bearing her name and your phone number, in case you get separated. ID bracelets work, too.

# The Rest of Your Vacation Stay

Outside of the clothing, toiletries, paperwork, medication, and electronic items you're accustomed to carrying on vacation, what else might you need during your stay in Orlando?

- this book!
- boarding passes
- hotel and car rental confirmation numbers
- tip and toll money
- proof of insurance
- stamps for postcards
- one dressy outfit for fine dining
- one or two bathing suits
- water shoes
- pool goggles
- extra socks
- workout clothes
- golf glove and golf shoes
- two pairs of comfortable walking shoes
- luggage tags for Disney's Magical Express
- sewing kit
- earplugs
- motion sickness medication
- safety pins
- nail clippers
- clothesline for wet items
- aloe for sunburns
- antibiotic ointment
- insect spray
- anti-itch cream
- Ziploc bags
- trash bags to store dirty clothing
- playing cards

- travel games
- night light or pen flash light
- chargers for phone, fitness device/watch, tablet, laptop
- earbuds or headphones
- laundry supplies
- Body Glide
- Moleskin
- stain stick
- wrinkle release spray
- stroller
- car seat
- swim diapers
- portable high chair
- baby monitor
- outlet covers

It's important to remember that airline mishaps can occur, and luggage gets misplaced. Be sure to pack extra clothes and toiletries in a carry-on bag, in addition to any prescription

Swimsuits, water shoes and sunscreen will come in handy at the Coronado Springs feature pool.

medicine you might need on your trip. If your child is old enough to handle her own bag, think about buying a backpack with wheels for her to pull through the airport and take on the plane, filled with the entertainment she'll want during the flights. And if you're heading to a theme park on the day of your arrival, have everyone put on their MagicBands before landing, so they're not forgotten later on.

# Food and Grocery Delivery

Our family typically stops at a grocery store after picking up a rental car in Orlando so we can buy the breakfast items and other groceries we'll need to enjoy light meals and snacks throughout our stay.

What if you aren't using a rental car during your time at Walt Disney World? Here are five options for getting the groceries you'll need: 1) pack food and kitchen items in your luggage, 2) ship a box of groceries to your hotel in advance, 3) buy groceries at your Walt Disney resort gift shop, at a hefty markup, 4) have groceries delivered to your resort once you check in, or 5) take a rideshare service or taxi to a nearby grocery store to do your own shopping.

Here are suggestions for what to take, when packing your own supplies:

- granola/breakfast bars
- Pop Tarts
- coffee
- tea bags
- non-dairy creamer
- powdered drink mix
- juice boxes
- sugar/sweetener
- packets of salt and pepper
- microwaveable popcorn
- fruit snacks
- peanut butter

- crackers
- chips/pretzels/trail mix
- instant soup mix
- plastic silverware
- paper plates
- paper towels
- plastic cups to bring to the pool

Most Disney World guests will elect to use a grocery delivery service when staying on Disney property, and for good reason: the online ordering process is simple, a drop-off time may be scheduled in advance, and you'll typically receive a text message or email notifying you of a successful delivery, at which time you can either retrieve your order from Bell Services in the resort lobby, or request room delivery. Tips may be left for the grocery deliverer through most websites or apps. Note that Disney will charge you $6 per delivery.

Shipping a box of groceries to your Disney resort—or to an offsite hotel that permits deliveries—is also an option for guests, though Disney will charge you that $6 fee on top of your shipping costs. To thwart the risk of a delivery delay, aim to have your box arrive a couple of days before check-in. You can also have boxes shipped to your Disney resort via Walmart, Amazon Pantry, and other vendors.

# Last-Minute Tips and Reminders

There's nothing like the week before a Walt Disney World vacation, as the months of anticipation build to a peak. It can also be a stressful time, filled with packing, last-minute errands, the effort of preparing a workplace and home for your absence, and getting kids on task for the upcoming trip. Throw in the extra planning a Walt Disney World vacation entails, and it can all become a bit overwhelming, even as your excitement mounts.

That's why I've broken down this chapter into a series of simple tips to follow, both for the days leading up to your vacation, and for your time at Walt Disney World.

So without further ado, let's dive in!

## The Week Before Your Trip

- Complete online check-in for your Disney resort. Doing so enables you to make room requests in advance of your stay and expedites the check-in process after your arrival. In fact, if you already have a MagicBand linked to your reservation, Disney can text you a room number on the day you arrive, allowing you to skip the lobby altogether and go straight to your room.

- If there was a hard-to-get ADR you were trying for, check again throughout the week, as many Disney guests will be tinkering with their itineraries. The same goes for FP+ reservations, too.

- Consult the weather forecast to know what awaits you in Orlando.

- Make sure you've asked the other members of your party for their must-do attractions, shows, and character meet-and-greets, so you have those prioritized.

- If you aren't using a rental car in Orlando, sign up for Uber or Lyft before you leave on vacation, especially if you have ADRs scheduled at Disney's resorts. Time really is money at Walt Disney World. Rideshare services can save you substantial travel time over Disney transportation, and new customers usually receive a free ride upon registering.

- Let your children know what to expect on the trip. If you're giving them a Disney gift card to use for souvenirs, tell them what they may spend in advance. If there are rides they can't experience because of height restrictions, be sure to prepare them ahead of time. And if you think they'll be scared of a specific attraction, look at a YouTube video together to gauge their level of interest or fear.

- Complete your car rental check-in online, so you can skip the airport counter.

- Pack a couple of days before the trip, so your final evening isn't as stressful. Aim to get as much rest as possible.

Like the dwarfs in Disney's popular Mine Train attraction, you'll be singing a happy tune on the way to Orlando.

- Don't forget to notify your bank card and credit card companies of your upcoming travels, to avoid any red flags on your account.
- Need a fun activity before the trip? Watch a Disney or Pixar film some evening together as a family to get everyone psyched up for the upcoming vacation.

# Day of Departure

- Pack your MagicBand and prescription medication in your carry-on luggage.
- Adjust your home's thermostat to an energy-saving setting during your absence. Many hot water heaters will have a "vacation" setting, too.
- Allot plenty of time for travel to the airport and for security. While you may be tempted to cut it close with an early flight, don't risk missing the first day of your vacation for thirty more minutes of sleep.
- If there's a lengthy drive to the airport in the morning, bring car pillows for the kids.
- While on your flight, review your park itineraries to make sure you're pleased with them. Familiarize yourself with the theme parks' layouts, and which Extra Magic Hours you'll utilize.
- Put on your MagicBands if traveling to a theme park or water park later that day.

# Arrival at Walt Disney World

- Whether traveling by car or via Magical Express, keep a lookout for the Walt Disney World welcome sign as you draw near the resort. Passing under it always feels like the "official" start of our Disney vacation. Nothing beats that feeling!
- If you're driving to a theme park first thing, and have completed online check-in at your Disney resort, you can have your MagicBand scanned by a parking lot attendant at any theme park, and he should wave you through.

Note I said "should." Occasionally, the system hits a snag. If you'd rather not have any doubts on this score, stop by your Disney resort before heading to a park.

- When arriving at your Disney resort before your room is ready, ask a lobby cast member to hold your luggage at Bell Services. Remember this tip on your departure day as well, should you need to check out of your room, but still want to spend time at the parks or Disney Springs.

- Be sure to pick up a "Celebration" button at your Disney resort desk, or at any Guest Relations theme park location, if marking a special occasion during your stay.

- Take a smartphone picture of your parking lot location (i.e., Villains: Captain Hook) before heading to the theme park, so you won't have trouble finding your car later.

- Pick up a Times Guide for entertainment and character meet-and-greet schedules when entering any of the four theme parks.

- You're finally at Walt Disney World! Take a moment to breathe it all in—and savor the feeling.

- Get on Disney's wifi network to avoid using cellular data.

- Check the My Disney Experience app for locations of attractions, shows, restrooms, restaurants, PhotoPass photographers, and character meet-and-greets. First filter the app for the theme park you're visiting. You can then see wait times for the relevant attractions. Make a note of when your first FP+ window opens up under "My Plans."

- Have a PhotoPass photographer take a group photo in front of each park's iconic landmark—Cinderella Castle in Magic Kingdom, the Epcot geosphere, the Tree of Life at Animal Kingdom, and the Chinese Theater at Hollywood Studios to commemorate this special moment.

# Food Tips

- Check the MDE app to see which table-service restaurant reservations may yet be available. Some ADRs can be booked last-minute.
- Cancel an ADR by midnight on the night before a meal, or face a $10/person cancellation fee. You may cancel via the app, or by calling (407) WDW-DINE.
- Don't forget about Mobile Ordering (see Step Eight).
- Adults may order off the kids' menu.
- Avoid crowds at counter-service restaurants by eating at off-peak times.
- Counter-service cashiers take orders on both sides of their registers, so if nobody is filling in one side, feel free to take the initiative.
- If you're on a Disney Dining Plan, the number of remaining dining credits in your account will be listed at the bottom of each meal's receipt. You can also consult the MDE app under "Check Dining Plan."
- If you're staying at a Disney resort, but aren't on the Disney Dining Plan, think about purchasing a refillable drink mug when visiting your resort's counter-service restaurant. If you think you'll drink more than six cups of soda, coffee, tea, or hot chocolate during your Disney resort stay, buying one will save you money.
- Tired some night and don't want to go out for dinner? You can have pizza delivered to your room at all Disney resorts (and likely at most offsite accommodations, too).
- If you're sticking to a budget, tally up your dining expenditures each day by keeping hold of your receipts. If you've been charging meals and other items to your room via your MagicBand, you can also hit "View Charges" on the MDE app.
- If you're using a Disney Dining Plan, don't forget to tip your servers.
- If there are snack credits remaining on your Dining Plan at the end of your vacation, buy some packaged snacks

to take home with you. The Main Street Confectionery in Magic Kingdom has a mouthwatering selection of tasty treats.

- Let your children know what to expect in terms of treats/ desserts each day, so you don't have to fend off their constant entreaties. If they get one big splurge a day, tell them that—and stick to it. The same goes for things like balloons and souvenirs.

# Ride Reminders

- Don't forget about the single-rider lines at Rock 'n' Roller Coaster, Expedition Everest, and Test Track.
- Make use of Disney's rider-switch program if you have a child who doesn't meet an attraction's height requirement, so that everyone else can enjoy it. (See Step Seven.)
- Search for a fourth, rolling FastPass selection on the MDE app as soon as you use your first three, either for the same park or for a different one when park hopping.
- Don't leave your belongings on the rides!
- Attraction lines lessen during the nightly fireworks shows, so if you've already seen the show—or don't care to—hit some popular rides then.
- Get into line right before park closing, when wait times are minimal.
- Be kind to Disney's cast members. Don't let your frustration over waits and crowds tip over into anger at them.
- If you're tired and needing a break, but don't want to leave the park just yet, head to a show or attraction that will get you off your feet. Some lucky folks are able to catch a quick nap at attractions like Carousel of Progress and Hall of Presidents in Magic Kingdom, or the American Adventure show and the French film in Epcot's World Showcase.
- If a ride goes down during your theme park visit, keep checking the MDE app to see if it's back up, instead of wasting time and energy traversing the park.

There's nothing "hidden" about this Mickey
on the floor of Epcot's aquarium.

# Miscellaneous Tips

- The best parks to visit on a rainy day are Magic Kingdom and the Future World section of Epcot. If it looks like constant showers in the forecast, consider switching your plans to one of these two parks. Animal Kingdom is the worst park to visit when rain clouds are threatening.

- The First Aid centers at Walt Disney World's theme parks are well stocked with free pain and cold medication, in addition to treating cuts, insect bites and stings, and eye irritations. They'll also hold any medication requiring refrigeration. Should you need further medical care, the Disney nurses have the numbers of nearby urgent-care centers.

- Keep track of your children at all times, especially during parades and after fireworks. Let your child know what to do in the event of a separation, and write your cell number on her ID tag, or on the inside of her MagicBand. For older children, prearrange a park meeting place in advance. Tell a younger child to find a Disney cast member ("the people wearing name tags") and explain she's lost. You should also contact a cast member in this eventuality. Disney has an efficient process for locating lost children throughout its theme parks, and Disney Security will be notified, stat. Often, a lost child is taken to a Baby Care Center or to First Aid before being reunited with his parents.

- If someone falls ill at a Disney resort, free transportation will be provided to a nearby urgent-care center. Should you need a prescription filled, and don't have a car, tell a cast member at the front desk and she'll arrange to have your prescription both filled and delivered.

- One way to stay healthy throughout your vacation is to remain hydrated. Don't neglect your water intake, especially during summer. Disney offers free water and ice at all counter-service locations.

- If you're a Disney resort guest, don't forget to have any theme park merchandise you buy sent back to your resort. If staying offsite, you can have souvenirs held at Package Pick-up at the front of the park.

- Another perk to being a Disney resort guest is the ability to request a wake-up call in the voice of a Disney character. Simply select the "Wake-up Call" button on your room phone to be guided through the process. Let your child answer the phone the next morning for a very special surprise.

- Keep a lookout for Hidden Mickeys!

- Take advantage of the full range of Disney transportation during your stay. Kids may find a ferry or monorail ride to be as novel as any theme park attraction.

- All Disney resorts offer Movies Under the Stars screenings on various nights, weather permitting. Check at the front desk for schedules.

- If you're near Cinderella Castle a half hour after Magic Kingdom's official closing, you'll get to experience the "Kiss Goodnight," a special sendoff that is the perfect topper to a most magical day.

- If you fall in love with Walt Disney World, and can foresee an opportunity to book another trip or two within the next year, think about upgrading your Magic Your Way ticket to an Annual Pass before the final day of your vacation at any Guest Relations booth.

# The Bounceback Offer

As your vacation draws to a close, it's normal to feel a little sad at the thought of leaving Walt Disney World. In fact, you might be tempted to flip this book back to the beginning and start planning your next trip! Post-Disney letdown is definitely a bummer.

Luckily, Disney's way ahead of you. That's why they offer their resort guests an extra incentive toward booking that next trip: the bounceback offer. What is it? Usually a good discount toward a room reservation or Magic Your Way package, available for select future dates. The one hitch? Your bounceback offer is only active while you're still a guest of Walt Disney World. The second after checking out, the clock strikes twelve, and the magic runs out.

Bounceback offers can often be found in your in-room welcome packet. If not, simply call down to the front desk and request details on all current bounceback offers. When contacting Disney's reservation system, inform the Disney cast member of the special discount before you put down the deposit (usually $200) toward your next vacation. Should you need to alter your plans later on, you can either modify the reservation (if your alternative dates aren't blacked out), or cancel without a penalty if negotiated far enough in advance.

I hope your Walt Disney World vacation was everything you dreamed it could be—and more! Remember to download your PhotoPass photos when you get home, so you can keep all those treasured memories right at your fingertips. And finally, let me offer my sincere thanks and appreciation for entrusting me with your one-of-a-kind Walt Disney World journey!

# About the Author

Sarah Hina is a writer, photographer, and Authorized Disney Vacation Planner. As a young girl, she enjoyed her family's yearly trips to Disneyland so much she couldn't bear to leave the park at night. Later, as a wife and mother of two kids, her passion for Disney's storytelling and innovation grew and strengthened through frequent family vacations to Walt Disney World, where she loved rediscovering the magic of Disney's theme parks through her children's eyes.

Now she's excited to share her experience with other Walt Disney World guests, in the hopes that her tips and insights will make their Disney memories as special as her own.

Visit Sarah's website, http://stepbystepwdw.com, for the latest Disney news.

Goodbye!

# ABOUT THEME PARK PRESS

Theme Park Press publishes books primarily about the Disney company, its history, culture, films, animation, and theme parks, as well as theme parks in general.

Our authors include noted historians, animators, Imagineers, and experts in the theme park industry.

We also publish many books by first-time authors, with topics ranging from fiction to theme park guides.

And we're always looking for new talent. If you'd like to write for us, or if you're interested in the many other titles in our catalog, please visit:

www.ThemeParkPress.com

. . . . . . . . . . . . . . . . . . . . . . . . . . . . . . . . . . . . . . . . . . . . .

## Theme Park Press Newsletter

Subscribe to our free email newsletter and enjoy:

- ◆ Free book downloads and giveaways
- ◆ Access to excerpts from our many books
- ◆ Announcements of forthcoming releases
- ◆ Exclusive additional content and chapters
- ◆ And more good stuff available nowhere else

To subscribe, visit www.ThemeParkPress.com, or send email to newsletter@themeparkpress.com.

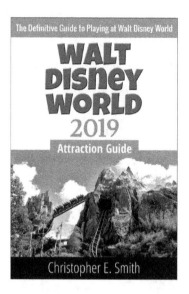

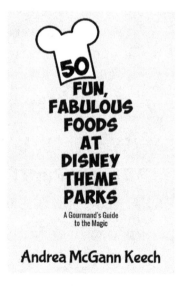

Read more about these books
and our many other titles at:

**www.ThemeParkPress.com**

CPSIA information can be obtained
at www.ICGtesting.com
Printed in the USA
LVHW031600060919
630200LV00010B/995/P

9 781683 902201